MW01223154

THE PERMISSION TO DREAM BOOK

Rebuilding Confidence From The Ground Up

Also by Mary Henington

The Goodness Calendar

THE PERMISSION TO DREAM BOOK

Rebuilding Confidence From The Ground Up

MARY HENINGTON

Copyright 2012 by Mary Henington

All rights reserved. No portion of this book may be reproduced, stored in a retrieval system, or transmitted in any form or by any means—electronic, mechanical, photocopy, recording, scanning, or other—except for brief quotations in critical reviews or articles, without the prior written permission of the publisher.

7 Stages of Grief by Jennie Wright, RN is used by permission of the author.

Bible translations quoted include:
King James Version
New King James Version
English Standard Version
The Complete Jewish Bible

THE MESSAGE: The Bible in Contemporary Language © 2002 by Eugene H. Peterson. All rights reserved. Used by permission.

New Living Translation ®, copyright © 1996, 2004 by Tyndale Charitable Trust. Used by permission of Tyndale House Publishers. All rights reserved.

The NET Bible®, Copyright © 1996-2006 by Biblical Studies Press, L.L.C., Dallas, Texas, www.bible.org. All rights reserved. Used by permission.

Library of Congress Cataloging-in-Publication Data

Henington, Mary.
The Permission To Dream Book: Rebuilding Confidence From The Ground Up / Mary Henington.

ISBN-13: 978-1483943985
ISBN-10: 1483943984

To Teri, Elinor and Dora,
without whom this book would not have happened

Contents

Disclaimer:

I am not a scientist. Therefore I am over-simplifying brain/mind, body, soul, and heart functions on purpose in the book for the sake of clarity for all of us. I believe what The Permission to Dream Book proposes holds true to the latest science, at least all that has been published in book format that I have read (see Reference list). I do not claim to have the whole picture of what's in the subconscious "mind," or how the body mind works in every detail. I have used this science to give my readers a fact-based understanding of the capabilities that are built into us as human beings. I know the premises and steps to reclaiming and discovering our dreams that are in The Permission to Dream Book work, because it's my life-recovery pathway also, and I've proved it out by living it.

೫ Preface

Some years ago, when I stepped away from a salaried job to start my own business and join the growing force of entrepreneurs in this country, I realized at the outset that my first year would probably be an intense learning curve, after nearly a lifetime of being a salaried employee. I read every success book I could lay my hands on, and networked with all the successful people I could find in my area and wherever my studies took me throughout the country.

Getting the business structured turned out to be the easy part, as new as it all was to me. I consider myself to be a lifetime learner and reasonably intelligent, and I loved the challenge of learning and implementing new skills. What threw me for a loop was finding several months into it that apparently something inside me was sabotaging what should have been successful effort. Where I should have been moving with confidence, I found myself hesitating and "feeling" uncertain.

In order to achieve success on the visible plain, I have had to dig deeply into my subconscious mind and uncover some painful truths about my internal programming. Dealing with negative expectations I didn't even realize were in me, and healing from the pain and losses in my life that were stuffed away unhealed or only partially healed has taken me some time. It is out of this process of personal growth that The Permission to Dream Book comes. This is not lecturing. These are life lessons I've learned and been changed by myself over the course of years; a journey I have walked out, and then formatted into a step-by-step process that I hope will give all who follow it an "I CAN." I can change, I can be successful, I can be happy again, I can live healthy. I can live the best life I can imagine.

‹₃₍₈ Introduction

"A journey of a thousand miles begins with just one step."

If life is a journey, then by definition, there is a starting point, a stretch of distance to be traveled, and a destination. There are any number of obstacles, points of interest, ups and downs, differences in climates, etc. between us and the ultimate outcome of our lives. We don't know at the beginning just what we will encounter. But a person starts down any road with an intention of going somewhere else, moving forward to reach a destination, some place ahead of and not presently all around them.

Of course, birth was our real starting point. And we'd already traveled a stretch on the road of life before we were able to have any say in the quality of our lives, or in the direction we were headed. That part of our road was not fun for many of us. It held obstacles and experiences that were painful, to say the least, and those things may still be giving us trouble.

Appearances are deceiving: As far as the world can tell, the structure of your life may look solid and stable, like this established brick building, while inside you is devastation and emptiness no one knows about.

Let's consider today as a new beginning and take a mental survey of where we are. It's possible to appear to the world around us like we have it all together, but be like the illustration shows, totally devastated inside. Only you know what's really in your heart and how the things you've lived through have affected you. People may not be able to tell by how you sound and how you act. But you know.

The starting point of our journey to our best life is the realization that there is something missing, the recognition that there *is* somewhere better I'd like to be than what I see happening in my life so far. That's a no-brainer, right?

"Thoughts are causes, and circumstances are effects: For every effect in your life, there is a thought or crop of thoughts that are responsible."
Tommy Newberry

If we're totally honest with ourselves, we know that a lot of the responsibility for where we are today is found in how we think, including how we think about ourselves in our deepest heart. So after the dual realization that there is something better I'd like for my life, and possibly my thinking patterns need some work, what do I do?

I believe that in order to get our best life, we have to deliberately dream it; and that we can begin moving into our best life simply *by* dreaming it. Dreaming is that powerful. Muhammad Ali said it this way: "Champions aren't made in the gyms. Champions are made from something they have deep inside them—a desire, a dream, a vision."

In this book, we'll define dreaming and lay out the steps to effective dreaming so we can get our minds around the HOW TO's. We will move into it one step at a time, laying a platform of truth and confidence under our feet while at the same time dealing with the obstacles and the losses that have kept us from travelling this pathway fully before. The first step on this section of our life journey is simple: keep reading the book.

It's not too late

If you've picked up this book feeling like you'd love to have a new way to get to a better life but you're stuck in the company of those who are hanging on by a thread, then be encouraged. Your best life is still possible. Reading The Permission to Dream Book, you will find life-changing new hope and some practical steps to get you moving from where you presently are and on the way into the best life you can possibly imagine.

To the person who dreams, "anything is possible." Right now, it's not important whether you believe this statement or not. I think you'd like to believe it, in that you're even reading about it. I hope by the end of the book, you'll believe it and be convinced no change is too big to accomplish in your life. There are no limits to how big you can imagine, to how high you can reach, how much of what was lost you can recover, and there is a way to do what seems impossible. We'll not only look at the steps to do it, we'll establish a foundation of scientific truth that will help us believe those steps are "do-able."

It is possible for YOU to live in your best life, either by reclaiming what you once wanted, or imagining it fresh for the first time. It is said that everyone needs at least one person who believes in you, in order to accomplish great things and overcome obstacles. I believe absolutely that you can do this. It's the reason I wrote the book.

Make this declaration with me:
What life has thrown at me so far is not who I am. I am not finished yet. I have the ability to make changes. I can imagine wonderful things, and move forward into them. There are good things ahead for me.

Section One:
Our Innate Ability to Dream

In the first section, we will look at the process of dreaming, breaking it down into four parts and examining each one separately.

০ৰ Chapter 1: The Bottom Line

*"Whether you think you can, or
whether you think you can't, you're right."*

Henry Ford

There is a profound truth in the statement by Henry Ford, that
whether we think we can or can't—either way—we're right.
Whatever we accomplish in life is rooted in what we believe we can
do. And whatever limitations we live under come from what we
believe we can't do. The fact that other people have had a hand in
forming these beliefs doesn't change the truth of the statement, that
my belief dictates what I am able or not able to do.

Whether I think I can or think I can't live a completely satisfying
life, the path to success or failure begins in my own beliefs, and
specifically, my *belief in myself* on a subconscious level.

There is nothing holding me back from living the most wildly
successful life I can imagine except my own self in my heart-deep,
invisible belief system. If I am living an unsatisfying life it is no one
else's fault, and it is not the fault of my circumstances. There is
nothing and no one else to take the blame for my dissatisfaction. My
"I can" or my "I can't" is rooted in my subconscious mind, in my
core beliefs. I am often surprised when an "I can't" pops out and
undermines something new I have decided I will do and consciously
think I can do.

"Well then," one might ask, "how do I find what I really believe in
my subconscious, since it's not easily visible or obvious, and is often
quite at odds with what I consciously think I can do, want to do or
plan to do?" A perfect example of this is our New Years'
resolutions. These are things we want to do, think we can do, and
fully plan to do. The fact that we don't last very long in performing
these good intentions is evidence that they are at odds with the
invisible belief system already established in our subconscious mind.

Something is getting in the way of our making changes to improve
our lives. Consciously chosen changes don't seem to last very long,

and the issue is usually not a lack of trying.

The real starting point

"We are fully living right now in what we believe." This is really frightening, yet it is literally true. Take a look at the way life is unfolding all around you and realize "THIS is what I believe on a very deep level within myself. This is what I think I can do, and what I think I deserve to have. I am not a prisoner of my circumstances; rather I am the *cause* of my circumstances. I am living *in this*, or *with this* (whatever "this" is), because of how I believe." What does that tell us about our beliefs?

First, our belief system *must be* somewhere other than the conscious mind, because we wouldn't consciously or deliberately choose a lot of what we're living in, if we're honest with ourselves about it. Who would deliberately choose to allow limitations to stand unchallenged in their lives, and keep them from moving continuously into better and better success?

Second, those invisible beliefs must be incredibly strong, able to override our conscious decisions and good intentions. The sad fact is that our own beliefs don't have to promote our well-being. They are not necessarily for our own good fortune—they can be and often are self-sabotaging or outright destructive. The dictionary defines sabotage as "to destroy, damage, or disrupt, especially by secret means." (1)

Take a look at Sally for instance. Sally was working toward her life goal, and making real progress. She was within weeks of getting the degree she needed to land her dream job. She went with a friend to a party to "let off some steam" and long story short, found herself in a relationship with a man who wanted all her attention. She ended up putting off finishing her degree until a "more convenient time" in the future. What happened here? Something within her caused her to self-sabotage her goal; a moment of uncertainty allowed her to make a heart choice her goal-oriented conscious brain should never have entertained, especially when she was so close to finishing. When I met her it had been decades since she met the man she eventually married, and her convenient time still had not shown up.

Test yourself for self-sabotaging behavior by asking yourself some of these questions: Am I focusing on what is not working, or what is not right about my life? Do I spend my time doing things that I don't even respect? Do I act impulsively and later find myself asking 'Why did I do that?!' Do I worry a lot about the future and what is going to happen or what may happen? Am I fearful? Does this keep me from taking new positive, confident action? Am I my own worst enemy?

If I do begin to get what I want, do I often lose it before long? Do I "put my foot in my mouth" and by my own words stop a relationship from going deeper, or a job opportunity from unfolding? Do I look for the flaws to new things that seem to be beginning to the point that I can't enjoy the good in them? Am I a glass half-empty person? Am I overly critical? Do I procrastinate? Do I compare myself with others, and feel like I come up short in the comparison? (2) If you said yes to even one of these questions, you too have invisible beliefs working contrary to and holding you back from your best life.

To find out what's in our belief systems, we have to know where to look. Beliefs are essentially thought sequences; therefore they exist in the mind. To enable us to find and, where necessary, change those established beliefs in the deep places of the mind which short-circuit good intentions and deliberately-set goals, let's start by learning a little about how the brain and the mind work.

The Science of the Brain and the Mind

"You are much more than the visible you. The brain is our primary control center, a fantastically complex organ containing billions of nerves that can simultaneously process information from our bodies, operate our internal organs, generate thoughts and emotions, store and recall memories, and control movement. Scientists have studied the brain for centuries and are nowhere near to fully understanding its intricacies."(3)

17

The human mind is amazing and mysterious. We have depths in our minds of which we are unaware as we go about our day-to-day lives. Scientists have been studying the brain mechanism and the human mind for hundreds of years, and yet their conclusions today as seen in the above quote from the National Geographic are that we're a long way from completely understanding how it works. Our brain is a mechanism, a living machine that runs our bodies. The physical brain is a wrinkled, jelly-like mass of fat and protein weighing about

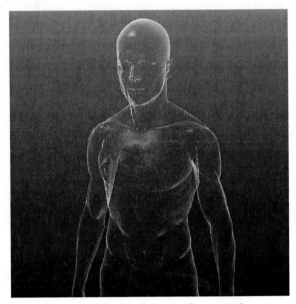

You are much more than the visible you. (4)

three pounds (1.4 kilograms). It is divided into four main areas called the brain stem, cerebellum, diencephalon, and cerebrum. The brain has areas of specialization, each area performing distinctly different jobs, at incredible speeds.

But beyond this tidy map, researchers now believe that multiple areas in the brain, the organs and the cells of our body, along with our nervous systems, our circulatory systems, our immune systems, and our endocrine systems each hold *parts* of the processes for what we've always thought of as exclusively brain/mind activities, (5) and the attempt to understand the mind's precise functioning is an ongoing science.

One example of how our understanding of the brain has changed:

until very recently, it was thought that adult brains didn't generate new brain cells, and once fully grown, when brain cells died, it was just too bad, so sad. "We used to think that by the age of five, you had all the brain cells you were going to get. Then neuroscientists discovered that your brain keeps growing when you're a teen and your frontal cortex doesn't stop developing until you're 25. But the new research shows that the growth of brain cells never stops—this replenishment, the influx of new brain cells, is going on throughout your entire life." (6) Today it's been proven that our brains never stop growing, and that to some degree what is lost through injury or illness can be regained. The brain has the capacity to rewire itself and form new neural pathways. "The brain is a plastic, living organ that can actually change its own structure and function, even into old age." (7)

Besides the obvious job of the brain mechanism in regulating the body, the brain has traditionally been thought to hold the workings of the "mind." Thomas Willis in the 1800's was the first one to suggest that the brain was the location of the mind. (8) Recent scientific discovery has shown that the mind is far different than we have speculated, The mind is much more than merely those thoughts of the brain beyond the parts used in maintaining the body's machine-works.

The mind is not just in the brain.

Neuroscience in the past three decades has exploded many of our ideas of brain/mind, by new science showing "the mind is the flow of information as it moves among the cells, organs, and systems of the body. The mind as we experience it is immaterial, yet it has a physical substrate, which is both the body and the brain. It may also be said to have a nonmaterial, nonphysical substrate that has to do with the flow of that information. The mind, then, is that which holds the network together, often acting below our consciousness, linking and coordinating the major systems and their organs and cells in an intelligently orchestrated symphony of life." (9) This elegant synopsis is the language of Dr. Candace Pert, the scientist who, with her first published findings in March 1973, shoved the ball of scientific understanding of the mind's location over the tip of an established understanding and got it started rolling downhill into new territory, where it's been picking up speed as it goes with continuing research results.

Dr. Pert says "We need to start thinking about how the mind manifests itself in various parts of the body...the concept of a network, stressing the interconnectedness of all systems of the organism, has a variety of ...implications. Mind doesn't dominate body, it *becomes* body—body and mind are one. The *mind* is in the body, in the same sense that the mind is in the brain, with all that that implies." (10) By convincingly meticulous science, she and fellow research scientists have shown that the processes of the conscious and the subconscious mind are distributed all over the body.

We are not just bodies with minds; we are 'bodyminds.' We are living networks of information-exchanging on a cellular level, incorporating our immune system, endocrine system, nervous system, circulatory system and brain into one whole intelligent, cohesively functioning human being. The nervous system with heart and brain, the circulatory system (heart, blood vessels, etc.), the endocrine system (gastrointestinal process), and the immune system each affect the whole body as they function, and yet they also form part of the "mind," in that *information* is stored in each of these systems.

Simply put, what we think affects us physically, and what we feel throughout our bodies affects what we think and remember.

The conscious mind

From this point on in the book, I'm going to talk about the function, not the location of the mind, because frankly I'm still processing the concept that my mind is in my whole body. It changes how I think of me. I believe that what I am saying lines up with the new science. I don't quote exact scientific sources on some parts of what I've included in the subconscious mind's workings, as they are my own thought-out conclusions. Time and more research will either bear me out scientifically, or better explain what I am writing about today.

Our conscious mind is the mind action we are most familiar with as we go about our everyday lives. "Our conscious mind is our awareness; it is responsible for logic and reasoning. It thinks, plans, reasons, calculates, determine results and makes decisions." (11)

The conscious, rational mind is that part of our brain that interacts with the physical world around us through our five senses, gathering and processing information. The mind captures information in snapshot format and records information in pictures. Have you ever suddenly "seen" the location of an item you'd misplaced, remembering by a mental picture where it is to be found?

There are thoughts that surface in our minds which we don't recognize as part of our conscious stream of thought, and that cannot be accounted for by whatever we are seeing, hearing or smelling. This indicates the existence of another part of the mind, somewhere outside conscious control which has an ability to speak into our awareness—an unconscious or subconscious mind. Our conscious mind not only doesn't control what goes on in this subconscious mind; in fact, it often is not aware of or doesn't remember what's in it. The subconscious mind, however, knows everything that's in our conscious mind, and even monitors what information *stays available* to the conscious mind on a day to day basis. For example, have you ever crammed for a test, and had all the information you needed to pass it at your fingertips? Where did all that information go a year later? Or even a week or two later?

The workings of our "mind" and especially our subconscious mind are still largely unknown territory and science hasn't fully explored the mind's capacities or gained a comprehensive understanding of its workings or the ramifications of its distribution throughout the body. This may well be the area of our soul and spirit, and both these words still tend to give scientists the "heebie-jeebies."

However, neuroscientists have been steadily working to break new ground of understanding in how the mind works. One branch of this field of scientific exploration is energy cardiology, which is beginning to explore how the heart factors into the "mind," storing memories in cells throughout the nervous system, thinking its own thoughts, and running things efficiently outside our brains. How the heart fits into our subconscious mind is a very interesting question. Where precisely in our physical brain and/or body the *center* of our subconscious mind exists, I couldn't definitively tell you. Both the conscious and subconscious minds' functions seem to be distributed all over the body.

We can sense there's much more to the mind than the surface we are seeing and experiencing in our conscious thoughts. My personal analogy is that the rational mind is like an ocean surface, and the subconscious mind is the ocean depths, off the charts, unmeasured. I know this subconscious mind exists, and that it has vastly greater capacities and strengths than our conscious mind, just like we are made aware of the power and immensity of ocean depths underneath us when we are out on the ocean surface and the winds pick up.

The subconscious mind

The hidden realm of the subconscious mind is the over-80% of our brain capacity that holds our heart and soul, that center of our being where our personality lives, where our motives come from, where our deepest thoughts and opinions are formed, where imagination runs freely, and where our personal truth—our individualized reality, that deeply-held belief system we were talking about—rules our lives. It's where the final word of what we will do comes from, like the word of an absolute king sitting on a throne in the center of our being.

Information is constantly going into and being dispersed out of our subconscious. Our subconscious mind retains EVERYTHING we've ever seen, heard, thought consciously, felt, intended, or done— science says information from even *before* the day we were born.

The subconscious collects data continuously, and it collects *all data as equal.* Think of it as more like a supercomputer than a sentient, differentiating person. Psychology calls it the adaptive unconscious, "a kind of giant computer that quickly and quietly processes a lot of the data we need in order to keep functioning as human beings." (12) Within the subconscious mind, there is no right or wrong, no real or unreal, no possible or impossible, no moral values, no important or not important emphasis given to the information it gathers. The mind doesn't discriminate; it just gathers equally weighted bits of information. It's much like the movie about the little robot who wanted to be alive, who was constantly asking for "INPUT." (13)

An example of this input: When we walk into a new location, our subconscious records thousands of information bits around us in phenomenal time, less than the blink of an eye—everything we see, everything we hear, the relationships of the objects in the room to each other, the relationships of everything in the room to us, as our internal perception quantifies it.

A staggering amount of information is streaming continually into the subconscious mind. "The subconscious mind processes some 20,000,000 environmental stimuli per second vs. 40 environmental stimuli interpreted by the conscious mind in the same second." (14) Since we don't live in a static world, fresh input is constantly presenting new interrelationships and new mental snapshots, new information even in familiar situations and locations, and the structure of our brain is changing every time we learn something new or have a new thought or memory. (15)

The "first impressions" that we experience in our new situations are actually *conclusions* based on all that real information taken into the subconscious mind at faster-than-supercomputer speed. Science calls this process "thin-slicing." (16)

Even though we can't access all the information that's already in our subconscious mind at will, we can deliberately think things through in our conscious mind any number of times and the conclusions we reason out will go into our subconscious mind each time as new "input." What we speak also goes into our subconscious mind as new information. Some of what we speak comes directly from the subconscious, and some comes out of conscious thought, but the moment we speak it, it becomes new input again entering into the subconscious mind. This works for us and against us, as we will see.

Some examples of what comes out of the subconscious mind are first impressions, dogma opinions (the ones that feel like they're set in concrete), inventive ideas, intuitions, answers to questions we've held in our conscious mind that connect-the-dots into a sudden understanding, deeply felt conclusions, solutions to problems, personality, self-image, and those flashes of inspiration we have first thing in the morning (or in the middle of the night) to a problem we've been mulling over. Subconscious "phenomena include repressed feelings, automatic skills, subliminal perceptions, thoughts, habits, and automatic reactions; and possibly also complexes, hidden phobias and desires." [17] Psychology sees subconscious processes being "expressed in dreams in a symbolical form, as well as in slips of the tongue and jokes." [18]

While I said that the subconscious mind acts like a sponge, collecting all information as equal, I need to clarify that there is one differentiation the subconscious mind does make—it recognizes when we've put importance on something by attaching strong emotion to it, and it logs that information in as a focus. Initially, importance is defined by the degree of emotion attached to an event coming into our memory for the first time. And once cataloged into memory, strong emotion holds that focus in place and it is handled differently than the rest of the mind's stored information. We'll come back to this concept later.

> *Because the subconscious mind does not
> distinguish between truth and fantasy,
> it accepts input without regard to present reality.* [19]

One of the most important facts about the subconscious mind as it relates to this book is that it recognizes no impossibilities, and like the quote from success coach Tommy Newberry says, it collects bits of information without distinguishing between truth or outright fantasy. It accepts input without paying any attention to our present "reality," thereby making unlimited dreams possible. There really is no impossible dream, based on *how the mind itself functions.*

The subconscious mind is only positive

If nothing else registers from the whole book, this next point alone can be life-changing. It was for me. The subconscious mind is *only positive.* There is no negative in it at all, in its capabilities or its operation. It doesn't even recognize the abstract ideas of NO, NOT, NEVER. These concepts simply do not register.

The subconscious mind doesn't differentiate between bits of information, remember? But it does recognize focus, based on the strong emotion attached to the information it receives. All our emotions have a positive purpose. Therefore anything that repeatedly comes attached to a strong emotion with NO, NOT, or NEVER is recognized as a focus because of the emotion. Since this is my mind and my focus, the subconscious drops off the NO, NOT, or NEVER it doesn't recognize and goes right to work to make that focus positively happen in my life.

I learned this process by seeing things I didn't like about my mother and vowing to myself *I will never be like my mother!* The subconscious received that as, *Oh, be like that!* and recognized the strong emotion attached to it, which made it a real FOCUS. One of the subconscious mind's jobs is to take our emotional focus as a directive, a command, and to make it happen.

One day I found myself looking in the mirror, seeing my mother, and asking myself *How on earth did this happen? I said I didn't want this.* My subconscious did exactly what I said, dropping off the NEVER, and giving me the very thing that made up my focus, that mental picture of my mother I strongly and emotionally didn't want.

What's in the subconscious mind?

There is growing evidence that our subconscious mind's control center is our heart. The heart *thinks.* "Science has recently discovered three startling new possibilities regarding how we think, feel, love, heal, and find meaning in our life. This research suggests that the heart thinks, cells remember, and that both of these processes are related to an as yet mysterious, extremely powerful, but very subtle energy with properties unlike any other known force. If the preliminary insights regarding these prospects continue to be verified, science may be taking the first tentative steps to understanding...the energy of the human spirit and the coded information that is the human soul." (20)

"Scientists...are pioneering research into the intelligence of the heart and the biochemical basis for memory in our cells." (21) In the introduction to his book *The Heart's Code*, Paul Pearsall, Ph.D., asks some very thought-provoking questions: "Is it possible that the heart has its own form of intelligence that, because of our evolved dependence on our brain for interpretation of our experiences, we are seldom aware of? Although very discreetly and in a much different way than the brain, can the heart literally perceive and react on its own to the outside world, and communicate an info-energetic code of that reaction through a network of tens of thousands of miles of vessels and 75 trillion cells, which serve not only as the circulatory system but as an energy and information emitting network? Have we been too 'brain focused' in our search for the mind, failing to see that the heart might be an informational and energetic cornerstone of a three-component 'Mind,' made up of a heart that energetically integrates the brilliantly adaptive brain with its miraculously self-healing body? Is what we refer to as the soul at least in part a set of info-energetic cellular memories, a kind of cellular soul program that is being constantly modified during the soul's brief stay in the physical body?" (22)

"Our understanding of the heart as a sentient organ is about where our understanding of the miraculous complexities of the brain was more than one hundred years ago. In comparison to the continuing rapid progress in study of the brain, learning about the heart as more than just a pump is developing much more slowly. The central hypotheses regarding information-carrying energy communicated by the heart were initially proposed by Drs. Gary E. Schwartz and Linda G. Russek. They are as clearly stated and testable as any other set of scientific suppositions, but the ideas of a "thinking" heart and information-carrying energy seem excessively difficult for many scientists to accept as starting points for study." (23)

What science is in varying stages of exploring, we are going to look at in an over-simplified manner for the sake of understanding. Our subconscious mind's functions can be viewed as a wheel with spokes—there's a central heart hub, and there are capacities which all respond to that hub and reach outward to accomplish a function, and interact with other parts of our bodies and minds. Chart 1 shows this relationship.

The heart is the command center of our mind and our life. The simple truth is that what's held in the heart affects every part of our lives, and whatever we have designated most important in our heart colors everything we say, do and believe. It affects our feelings, our choices, what we imagine and remember and what we continue to focus on.

We have the ability to "set our hearts" on something we want. It begins with a choice. We choose what we think will make us happy, and that is what directs our lives from our hearts. Whatever person, idea or thing we think will satisfy us is essentially what we have put at the position of control in our lives, as if our heart had a throne, and that person, thing or idea was sitting on it. This positioning over time is integrated into our core identity and our life rotates around it. It effectively rules us.

Some people think fame will satisfy, or wealth, and the pursuit of those things shapes their lives. Some people put a spouse or a significant other in that position, which never seems to work, maybe because none of us is as self-sacrificing as this role needs us to be in another person's life. Some of us put an ideology in this place. An extreme example: after World War II the Russian leaders chose communism, and many people bought into the same ideology. The whole world witnessed how disastrously that worked.

These are the capacities we will look at, which are all found in the subconscious mind:

1. **Self-awareness**: the quintessential quality that makes us human.

2. **A memory bank**: the archives of all our memories.

3. **Imagination**: where new ideas are explored and memory is revisited.

4. **Conscience**: our moral map, our value system regulator.

5. **Independent will**: our ability to decide—all choices, decisions and judgments are formed here.

6. **Desires and feelings**: our emotional opinions and reactions.

Chart 1: The subconscious mind

The heart's job is to keep our bodies and minds working in harmony for our well-being and sanity. We all have in us a personalized "TRUTH." This is the rulebook our heart uses in keeping us integrated and on course. The abilities of our subconscious mind both affect the heart and take orders from the heart; together they make up this place of individualized truth. This is our central belief system, our reality, our life truth. It comes from many sources: observation and conclusions taken to heart (often a subconscious process), from teaching, from wounds with their accompanying messages, from labels people have laid on us and with which we have over time come to agree. You get the picture.

Our world view is seen through this composite, even though it's deeply embedded in our subconscious mind, far out of reach of our conscious awareness. Our belief systems act as life judges, critiquing every event, every plan, holding everything up against the standard of "my true identity as I *believe* it to be." And our heart's job, which is to keep us sane according to our belief system, allows it to use its ability to veto and override any outcome to our activities which opposes that belief system.

Remembering that the subconscious doesn't differentiate between real or not real, it doesn't make any difference if our reality is rooted in actual truth or not. Our reality is *our truth* and it affects everything we do and every decision we make. It affects how we think about ourselves and how successful we presently are or ever will be. This may be completely at odds with our conscious plans, our ambitions for ourselves, our talents and our abilities.

Simply put, if our life truth is based on wrong information, we will be seeing life wrong, living with less than our best life, living below our potential. We have to make some drastic changes to interrupt this growing deposit of wrong, self-sabotaging, highly emotional "truth" in our subconscious minds. We want to do what is necessary to unseat the despot on our heart's throne and bring in some positive goodness and put a good expectation there instead, something that will cooperate with our new dreams for our best life, instead of undermining our efforts to get there.

If we are not living a satisfying life, it isn't our activities we have to change first—it's our belief systems. Remember that we are fully living right now in *what we believe*, so to make lasting life changes it is necessary to begin by changing our subconscious heart beliefs. Permanent change does not come merely by changing behavior. It must come from changing our belief system, our faulty reality, and unseating the emotional memories by which that reality is "stuck." We'll come back to this in Chapter 9, and learn how to correct what's in our belief systems, even if we've discovered it to be completely messed up.

How Dreams are created

Dreams are formed in our subconscious mind, mixing hope with our imagination and desire, and projecting ahead into the future an "It could happen to me." By imagining it, picturing and coming to want it fiercely, choosing to see ourselves in it and talking like we're already there, we can literally change the course of our life and rewrite our future. We will find ourselves making new choices and deliberately thinking and declaring the things that will be part of our dream, getting emotionally involved with the things we're declaring that are nowhere in sight yet. And when our Dream seems to coalesce and materialize around us we will be surprised by how the pieces are coming together seemingly out of nowhere.

Let's divide the process of dreaming into four components: hope, imagination, choice, and deliberate speaking with strong emotion. We'll examine each component separately, while at the same time exploring the capacities we have as human beings which enable us all to use these components and successfully dream.

Building a dream from the bottom up.

Let's start at rock bottom, and work up to a completed formula for successful dreaming. The first element of a dream is hope. Every human being has a measure of hope. Hope is defined as a fiercely strong, positive emotion that focuses only on the future. The dictionary says hope confidently believes, usually for good reasons that an event may occur, and actively expects that it will. Hope works like a telescope, bringing what is invisible in the future into a clear, up-close view.

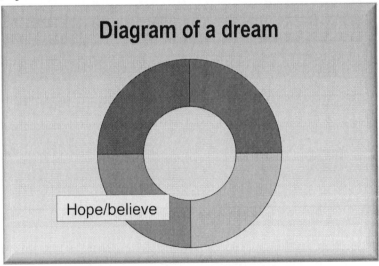

Chart 2: The first element of dreaming is hope

Hope is the root *emotion* of dreaming. Hope personalizes our expectations, and it is what tells us "that good thing I'm anticipating in the future is *possible for me*." Hope is a real motivator.

Hope is the feeling that what I want is not only possible for me, it's *likely* to happen. It's the feeling that events will turn out for the best. Hope means to look forward to something with desire and reasonable confidence. (24)

Hope is not pie-in-the-sky wishful thinking; it's not things we wish for but have no confidence in them actually happening. Hope only focuses on that which we believe is likely to happen. I have to believe it's possible *for me*, in order for hope to be a real and effective motivator.

How hope becomes depleted.

Hope is such a positive and good quality, why doesn't everyone have a strong hope motivation? What happens to it? What affects the strength of our hope?

If what we're hoping for ourselves is delayed, we will be disappointed. Too much disappointment makes us sick at heart and both delays and disappointments adversely affect the level of our hope. The heart perceives continual disappointments and delays as "If what I am expecting to satisfy me is not coming soon, then maybe rather than merely being delayed, it's being denied to me."

From this point, momentum picks up in decreasing our hope, like water draining out of a hole. Throw in some negative comments, some criticisms from those who observe our lives and we begin to question the value of what we were hoping. We begin to doubt our original hope; we start to wonder "Is it really possible?" It's amazing how quickly additional negative talk accumulates then, including our own self talk. We start talking ourselves out of our hope internally, to protect ourselves from the pain of further disappointment.

And then shame kicks in, telling us we're not worth what we were hoping for anyway. And limitations solidify, doubt and fear grow, and eventually our hope is completely engulfed. Our expectation becomes something fearful, rather than hope-full.

What happens when we don't have much hope?

Whereas healthy hope is our positive, possibility-seeing, forward-looking emotion, when it's full of fear, it looks forward to positively fearful possibilities. The counterpart of hope, its "dark side" is dread. Picturing worst-case scenarios is one way fear suggests possibilities. Repeating that pictured possibility in our imaginations (and it repeats like a broken record, doesn't it?) builds up a whale of a big emotional response, which then gives a totally awful focus to our subconscious. And our subconscious goes to work to make our focus happen. Which in turn makes us more fearful, and we picture even worse worst-case scenarios. It escalates all out of control. It's a vicious cycle.

> *"Man can live about forty days without food,*
> *about three days without water,*
> *about eight minutes without air,*
> *but only for one second without hope."*

Anonymous

Only I can determine whether my hope is strong enough to propel me into my best life, or whether my current hope level is low, and needs to be built up. There's a bottom line test for hope: Am I still breathing? *"There is hope only for the living."* (25)

This is our bottom line, the platform from which we can begin to build our best life: **If I'm alive, there is hope for me**. And we can choose to build up our hope, rather than allow it to continue to be depleted. Even though it seems an impossible distance between simply breathing and our best life, the absolute truth is that just being alive makes it possible for me.

Hope has a stubborn strength, it "hopes against hope." Hope deals with the invisible future—when there is no visible evidence yet of the expected possibility, hope still expects it. The "poster child" for hoping against hope is the Hebrew patriarch Abraham. He was promised a son when he was 80 years old, and he had to live with only a promise for 20 years. That seems like a long time to hope. The Bible says "Even when there was no reason for hope, Abraham kept hoping—believing that he would become the father of many nations." (26)

"Hope begins in the dark, the stubborn hope that if you just show up and try to do the right thing, the dawn will come. You wait and watch and work: you don't give up. "

Anne Lamott

Abraham's wife Sarah was almost 90 when she was told she'd have a son soon, and she laughed outright, knowing she was long past the time of childbearing. Yet what looked like an obvious impossibility did happen and Abraham and Sarah's son Isaac was born the next year.

Declaration #1: If I'm breathing, it's my absolute right to have hope.

⛥ Chapter 2: Hope grows

To dream our way into our best life, it is mandatory we have a strong and healthy hope that enables us to keep looking forward, thinking about the possibilities ahead of us. We have seen how hope can be depleted. So how do we increase our hope?

It is a universal law that everything living grows. (1) Growth may be either in a positive or negative direction, but it is *increase* in one direction or the other. Therefore our emotional capacities are growing, our imagination storehouses of memories are growing, the weight of evidence for our belief systems is accumulating within our subconscious minds, and we are becoming more who we are every day. One example I witnessed firsthand—my father was always a tease; he loved to stir it up a bit and get into a friendly argument. Most of his life his good-natured teasing was just part of who he was, and enjoyable to everyone around him. But in his old age he became more argumentative and often downright "ornery." The point is, every capacity and characteristic we have is continually growing as long as we're alive.

We need to use this universal law and "sow" some new belief-changing seeds into our subconscious minds. We need to sow into our hope. And we need to do it with the mindset that in the same way as when we're planting literal seeds, there will be a resulting "harvest" in time. Like the Bible says "the one plowing and threshing ought to work in hope of enjoying the harvest." (2) The new activities we'll be doing to build our hope may seem like very small things, but they are seeds, and all seeds start smaller than their end result will be. Seeds *grow*.

However, the seeds we plant don't produce their harvest overnight. There is a waiting period before any new life is even visible above ground. This will be true for a strengthened hope—we must persist in doing the activity that is building it without expecting the instant gratification of increased hope.

Learn to do something and consider it seed, or water on an already planted seed, and be okay with it, continuing to regard it as growing even though you can't see the evidence of its growth yet. Hope tells us that although a thing is not visible yet, it is still *real*. If we refuse to embrace hope's invisible expectations as real and important to us, we are relegating ourselves to live by our circumstances. The problem with that lifestyle is that our circumstances don't remain stable either; they are growing and changing along with everything else.

Seed sprouting (3)

Hope is expectation. Hope is what I expect to satisfy me when it comes, and hope puts confident belief into its coming. When hope grows strong and healthy, it will activate a confidence that propels us into action. Hope by its nature always expects the invisible to materialize in real time, and watches along with our confidence capacity for evidence of the expectation getting nearer. Picture your confidence as a collector carrying a basket, arm in arm with your hope, going around looking for bits of evidence of the thing hope is expecting to see happen. Hope says "that's part of what I'm looking for," and into confidence's basket it goes. When enough evidence has been collected, we will have such a burst of confidence we'll find ourselves *doing* things we could only think about before.

Building hope.

Build hope deliberately starting right now—by planting some new things in your life. The following are actions, but they have the same effect as seeds we can sow in the garden, in that they will bring a "crop" of increased hope:

1. Make a commitment to yourself and to the process of moving forward into your best life (*see Chart 3*). We do not live our best life because someone else thinks we should, nor will we get there unless we commit ourselves to do whatever it takes. Re-affirm this commitment over and over and over again, until it becomes part of your heart-deep "truth."

2. Start a list of the absolute truths that make the solid foundation for your dream.

3. Start an Evidence Journal. When you see or think something that aligns with your best life as you're imagining it, write it down; include quotes, life examples, ideas, visual bits that spoke to you, etc. Don't leave it only to your hope to gather the evidence. Be a partner in this, and hope will be able to recognize the evidence of your satisfying life approaching much more readily.

4. Examine your heart. Pay attention to why you do what you do— start examining your own motives. Evaluate your motives for indications of what you really value, and ask yourself "Does this contribute to my reaching my best life, or is this hindering me?"

5. Speak your new truths out loud to yourself every day. (*Feel free to jump ahead in the book to* Chapter 7 *for a template of how to write effective declarations.*) Pull up these declarations and say them any time during the day when things threaten to get out of hand.

6. Use the declarations at the end of each chapter of Permission to Dream, and speak them to yourself out loud daily. This will not be wasted effort. The more often you hear yourself saying them, the more you will believe what you're saying, and the sooner a crop of that thing will show up.

7. Read material that builds your hope. Read the life stories of great men and women who became what you are aiming to become, or

who succeeded wildly in what they did. It is said that success breeds success. Encourage yourself with other people's successes.

8. Begin using "I CAN" language with yourself. Whether your heart argues with this or not, start saying "I can do it!" We have a huge underground reservoir of "I CAN'T" in us, or we would already be doing whatever it is we're arguing about within ourselves. Even though it takes 11 positive statements to counteract one negative statement, one drop of water in the form of one simple I CAN continually dripping into our core beliefs will eventually wear away the rock of I CAN'T.

9. Connect with the God of Hope. He is the one who created humanity for success, and put amazing capacities within us to enable us to succeed. It's in the heart of God for us to have our best life. "For I know the thoughts that I think toward you, says the LORD, thoughts of peace and not of evil, to give you a future and a hope." (4) Doesn't this make you the tiniest bit curious to know what he might have in mind for you?

Examine our own heart

If what we put our hope in is what we live for, in a sense it's our heart's treasure. Ask yourself, "Where have I put my hope in the past? What do I value the most? What do I expect to satisfy me? Do I believe this is possible for me?" Whatever it is, *that* is your hope.

Where your treasure is, there will your heart be also. (5)

Because our heart is in the subconscious part of us, examining what's in it is like asking the librarian for a book that's not out on the conscious mind bookshelves. We may have to wait for our heart to bring us the answer, and tell us what it wants.

I found a little article online that outlined one way to hear what your heart is telling you: "One simple way to get out of your head and into your heart is to sit quietly with your hand on your heart, and take in several slow deep gentle breaths. Then allow yourself to think of someone or something that you truly love (this helps you to

37

strengthen your connection to your heart). From this place silently ask yourself what you want, and then listen for the answer. You may want to ask this question several times in order to access the deepest part of yourself and reveal the true desire of your heart. The answer may come to you as a word, an image, or a thought." (6) But the answer will come. You will know what your heart hopes in, if you ask yourself the question and get quiet enough to listen to your heart's gentle, quiet voice. When your heart answers and you realize what you have put your hope in, ask yourself, "Is that a good thing to hope in or not? Will it move me closer to my best life? Will it truly satisfy me?"

Very often the mothers to whom I teach this material have a hard time seeing past their children's welfare to the life they themselves will be fully satisfied in living. Many times they are focused only on the immediate future, providing a safe home for their children. Yet childrearing is a job you work yourself out of, if you're successful at it, and you have years to fill at the end of the "children season." So try to see beyond the children you love: what will you be happy doing for the rest of your life? What will use all your potential and benefit both you and the world you live in?

We put our hope in what we count on to satisfy us and our hope is what tells us it is possible for us. We have the ability to place our hope in a person, like "the love of our life," or in a thing, like money, education, success or fame, etc. Don't continue to "pin your hopes" on things that are obviously not working. Instead, *put* your hope in something that has the ability to truly satisfy. Keep listening to your own heart, to discover where you and your heart agree, and where you've been disagreeing, so you can build your best future in a whole-life harmony.

The more we feed our hope, the more it grows into confidence.

Confidence is crucial to success of any kind. It's when our hope has built itself into the compelling confidence that moves us into action that we see the real benefit of building our hope. This mature confidence is how we step out into new things, how we succeed.

Confidence is what Olympic athletes take into the arena of their sport, as much or more than their skill. One athlete said: "This game is not about winning, it is about one thing, confidence... That's the only thing you need, it's not skill, it's not a plan, it's confidence." (7) Carl Lewis said it another way: "If you don't have confidence, you'll always find a way not to win."

The ability to move forward in confidence is universal to human beings. It's built into us. Every person who has ever lived has this ability. Different people have different levels of confidence. One person may find it a major undertaking just to confidently walk out of the house to the mailbox and back again. That wouldn't seem like a big confidence placed alongside the Olympic athlete confidently competing in his excellence, yet they are both "I CAN" in action.

Where we are in our confidence level is something we must determine for ourselves. Only I can know how near my hope is in strength and maturity to the confidence that will get my feet moving.

To recap this chapter, what we put our belief in to satisfy us is what we have placed in our heart of hearts. From that center, all our life is arranged; every part of our life is affected by our hope. Hope ties us to the center, the core of our life, and it grounds us. Our hope keeps us focused. It holds our thoughts, feelings and even our decisions from being scattered. It saves us from acting like a chicken with its head cut off—lots of frantic activity, but already dead with no future. With the right focus for our hope, there is balance to our life. All the different facets of our life can function in harmony, complementing each other, like well-tuned machinery. But if we put our hope in the wrong things, and make the wrong things our heart's "treasure," our life cannot help but be out of balance.

Put your hope in God. He makes balance possible. (8)

Declaration #2: I am rebuilding my hope and it will grow stronger.

My Commitment to Myself

I, _____

am a unique human being. I don't have to imitate anyone to be valuable.

I have abilities and dreams that are important to me and to the world I live in. I choose to put my wholehearted effort into accomplishing my dreams, starting right now.

I will not allow the distractions of life to keep me from this. There are ways to handle obstacles and distractions, and I will find them. If anybody else got their dream, even in the face of what looked like impossibilities—and I know people have done this—then I can too.

I give myself permission to go after my dreams and live my best life. I can do this.

Signed on this ___19___ day of ___Jan___, 2019

Kelli Maloney
My signature

Chart 3

ೞೞ Chapter 3: The Building Blocks of Our Dream

Step two of the dreaming process is to imagine.

In the last chapter, we touched on how imagination shows us pictures of either our hopes or our fears. Let's see how it works for us in dreaming.

Imagination is our ability to form mental images or concepts of things not touched, seen, smelled, tasted or heard. Our imagination gives us the ability to confront and deal with reality by using the creative power of the mind; it's our resourcefulness. Imagination works both with mental pictures of past or future things, and with ideas of things that have never existed yet in our experience.

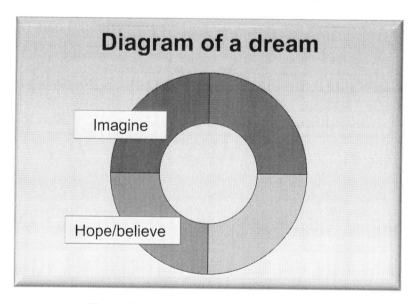

Chart 4: Second component of a dream is Imagine.

When I was growing up, I read a sci-fi story about a little girl in grade school, whose mother warned her teacher to be careful what she taught the child, because she was "the believing kind." Whatever she got into her imagination manifested itself in reality. [1] Even in a short story that had chilling implications, but the message to us is that our imagination is much more powerful than we may realize.

Imagination has two very different parts.

The first part of our imagination is the reproductive imagination. It's defined as "the power of reproducing images stored in the memory under the suggestion of associated images." (2) In other words, memories which are triggered by something similar happening currently. Our reproductive imagination pulls up memories and tells us that because events happened this way before, we can expect that same thing or something very similar to happen again.

The reproductive imagination takes every current situation and forecasts outcomes based in a large part on the outcome of similar significant moments in our past. Have you ever had a "déjà vu" experience? Your reproductive imagination is speaking out.

Our traumatic life events are usually recorded memory Moments with a capital M. Those moments in our history leave strong markers in the landscape of our reproductive memory. I call them "signposts." Each time our memory plays back that event, we have a fresh feeling about it, and that feeling goes into the subconscious mind as new information, and adds to the recorded size of the signpost memory. The more emotion that's attached to the memory, and the more often we "remember" it, and feel a fresh twinge of emotion about it, the bigger the signpost, and therefore the more influence it will have on our present and future situations.

Your imagination works backwards and it works forwards.

"It's a poor sort of memory that only works backwards."
Lewis Carroll

The second part of our imagination is the creative imagination. It's defined as "the power of recombining former experiences in the creation of new images directed at a specific goal or aiding in solution of problems." (3) This is like throwing up a handful of jigsaw puzzle pieces that make up one of our signpost memory pictures, and then, instead of feeling locked in to putting the pieces where they fit together before, using them to create a completely new picture.

Creative imagination is what gives us the ability to confront our flawed belief system and insert different possibilities into our life using the creative power of the mind. In the face of a situation similar to a less-than-satisfying signpost moment in our past, we can think up different possibilities as potential outcomes instead of settling for an outcome like whatever happened before, thereby opening up a more positive future for ourselves.

Every drop of our creative imagination is full of glittering possibilities. This is the realm of unlimited possibilities, where anything we can get our mind around becomes possible. This is imagination that's not limited to information received through the five natural senses, from experience, or from circumstances. This is where we move out of past failures and the sense of trapped hopelessness that clings to their memory, and into a place where we start thinking "Now, how can we make this thing happen?" This is possibility thinking. This is where our imagination takes off, gets airborne, and flies high.

Obviously we need a paradigm shift in our imaginations. A paradigm shift is merely a change from one way of thinking to another, but it can be sudden and provide an "aha" moment of realization. It can also be a shift in perception that affects a whole culture for the rest of time—as in the paradigm shift from candle and lamp light to electric light, or the introduction of the printing press to produce books, instead of laboriously hand-lettering every book copy. We need some "aha" moments in our *memories vs. possibilities* thinking. We need to detach from how it *was* to free ourselves to imagine how it *could be* in our futures.

Refuse to dwell on what gets regurgitated out of our reproductive imagination. There is a way to defuse those emotionally-powerful Signposts and rip our attention out of the past, allowing us to begin focusing on forward-thinking and imagining. (*See Chapter 13.*)

Anything is possible in the creative imagination.

In the same way that if we're alive, we are able to hope, it is science that our mind has the ability for unlimited imagination.

*The ultimate creative capacity of your brain may be,
for all practical purposes, INFINITE.*

Dr. W. Ross Adey—Brain Research Institute UCLA

Dr. W. Ross Adey was the Director of the Space Biology Laboratory at the UCLA Brain Research Institute (BRI) between 1961 and 1974. Chris Evans, the current director of BRI says "Understanding the brain is the greatest frontier in modern life science and medicine." (4) These statements are the voice of science. Our ability to imagine is so much greater than the best "imaginer" in all of humanity has ever fully exercised.

Imagination is part of our subconscious mind, yet we consciously choose to use it. It's like turning on a light switch. The electricity is generated somewhere else, but we have conscious use of the light. Since our imagination is primarily part of our subconscious mind, nearly everything that we imagine, once conceived in mind, is received back simply as new input, with equal emphasis and does not register as either possible or impossible. There is no real or unreal. Repetition of our imagined concept coupled with a strong emotion is what can pull it into reality, whether it's the limitations of "impossible, it never turns out like that for me" coming out of our reproductive imagination or it's a new possibility that's never been done before coming out of our creative imagination. Ask yourself, Where do I want my oh-so-effective imagination to do its work, pulling my past into my future, or opening up new ideas and possibilities?

Since our subconscious mind does not recognize the concept of impossible, we need to re-evaluate the limitations we have lived with, and what we have thought of as impossible for ourselves. The dictionary defines impossible as:

1. Not possible, incapable of having existence or of occurring.

2. Unable to be done, performed, effected, etc.
   Not capable of being accomplished

3. Utterly impractical—an impossible plan.

4. Hopelessly unsuitable, difficult, or objectionable. Unacceptable or intolerable. (5)

In other words, totally unlikely. You choose—what would you rather have picturing your future, your possibility-producing creative imagination, or your limitation-producing reproductive imagination, telling you all the reasons you "can't?"

> *"Alice laughed. 'There's no use trying,' she said.*
> *'One can't believe impossible things.'*
> *'I daresay you haven't had much practice,' said the Queen.*
> *'When I was your age, I always did it half an hour a day.*
> *Why, sometimes, I've believed as many*
> *as six impossible things before breakfast.'"*
>
> Lewis Carroll, Alice in Wonderland

Take a moment and look at the "impossible" imaginary ideas of some people in history: The great renaissance painter Leonardo da Vinci left notebooks full of his imaginations sketched out. Some of what was creative imagination for him in the fifteenth century became commonplace equipment in the twentieth century. He imagined an armored car that gave us the basis for the modern tank. He imagined the helicopter, scuba gear, robots, a flying machine (airplane) and a self-propelled cart (motorized car), and a parachute.

> *"The Wright brother flew right through the*
> *smoke screen of impossibility."*
>
> Charles F Kettering

How many thousands of years was it accepted as undeniable truth that man could not fly? People said "If man was supposed to fly, he would have wings!" with absolute conviction. In 1903 when Wilber and Orville Wright flew the first airplane, the idea that it was impossible for man to fly was such a fixed understanding that Scientific American suggested the flight was a hoax, and for 5 years officials in Washington, D.C. didn't believe the Wright brothers' airplane had really flown.

Thomas Edison invented thousands of things; in his lifetime he held

1093 patents for his inventions. It probably seemed impossible to get a practical working light bulb in 1879 when he was somewhere in the middle of the two thousand tries and failures it took to come up with the right material to make it work. Have you tried *anything* more than1900 times without giving up?

Besides finding the right kind of filament, Edison also had to create a total of seven system elements that were critical to the practical application of electric lights as an alternative to the gas lights that were prevalent in his day. These were the development of the parallel circuit, a durable light bulb, an improved dynamo, the underground conductor network, the devices for maintaining constant voltage, safety fuses and insulating materials, and light sockets with on-off switches. Every one of these elements had to be first invented and then, through careful trial and error, developed into practical, reproducible components. (6)

★ *"Impossible situations can become possible miracles."*
Robert H Schuller

The French author and father of science fiction, Jules Verne, left us a number of his fantastic imaginations, which have been realized in our time as submarines, lunar modules, solar sails, skywriting, videoconferencing technology, the Taser, and television newscasts.

The author H.G. Wells wrote about people communicating almost entirely by wireless telephones and voice mail, decades before the advent of the first cell phone or answering machine.

He also imagined the time machine, which no one has managed to make workable yet, and which therefore still resides in the pool of the "impossible." Wells also thought up a "heat ray" to kill off invading Martians in his *The War of the Worlds,* published in 1898.

Today the U.S. military's more benign version of a heat ray mounts on a truck and uses microwave radiation to make crowds feel uncomfortable enough to disperse.

Other impossible dreamers are imagining anti-gravity vehicles, fuel-free energy, invisibility cloaks, terraforming, energy shields, bionics. (7) What imaginations of today will be the commonplace technology of the world tomorrow? How many failures will be involved in the trial and error process of their implementation?

> *What is now proved was once imagined.*
>
> William Blake

These are just a few examples. The creative imagination is all about possibilities. Human beings are created with a desire to think outside the box, to push against the limits of possibility and move into new territory formerly thought impossible. It exhilarates us, it fulfills us.

Let's make a paradigm shift in the way we use our imaginations. Stop giving our attention to our reproductive imagination, allowing it to focus on what has already been, which tends to reproduce failure over and over again in our lives. Begin to think possibilities.

Look at the impossible differently

Look at impossible situations with a different focus. Look at them as opportunities. If we relentlessly think possibilities, our most awful moments can be turned around. There are still miracles. They happen all the time. I'll tell you about just a couple of the many I've seen. I am going to tell you some of the first ones I experienced, when I was new to my faith, and didn't know what to expect.

> *"I am realistic. I expect miracles."*
>
> Wayne Dyer

The first miracle I ever saw happened when I was still a teenager. I went to a prayer meeting in Seattle with a friend, and while we were there, a middle-aged lady in a wheelchair asked for prayer. She had worked in a mental institution, and been attacked some years before, and her spine was all twisted (visibly) so that she was unable to sit straight, or to stand up and walk. Because this was my first time seeing the miraculous, even though I no longer remember the names of the people involved, I can still see in my mind's eye the lady straightening up when she was prayed for, the shocked look on her face, and the way she jumped up out of her wheelchair and started cavorting around the room, dancing and jumping up and down, and clearly moving freely without pain. One moment visibly hunched over and twisted sideways, the next *straight*, and shouting with the joy of it.

A school friend of mine lived in Oregon, and one day found herself home alone with a big problem. She got bit on the neck by a black widow spider, and it was swelling up fast. No one was around to take her to the hospital, and you don't have a lot of time after being bitten to play around. She called someone to pray for her, and he said to put the phone receiver over the bite on her neck. She did, and the man spoke right to the bite mark apparently, because immediately the swelling began going down, until it was all gone.

This same friend went to the prayer meetings with me where the lady in a wheelchair got healed. At another meeting, she asked me to go with her to ask the leader of the meeting to pray for a lump on her arm. The leader turned to me, and said "Put your hand on the lump, and tell it to be gone." I did, and he put his hand over mine as I spoke. And I felt that lump dissolve under my hand. When I moved my hand and we looked—no lump. That incident stands out in my memory, because it was the first time I personally participated in the miraculous.

I don't remember where this next incident took place exactly, except that it was a church setting somewhere in the Seattle area. A lady asked for prayer; she limped and had back pain continually because of the limp. The leader of the meeting asked her to sit down with both legs stretched straight out before her, and he moved another straight-backed chair into position under her legs. I watched her one leg, clearly shorter than the other one by about two inches, grow to the same length as her other leg in the space of about 15 seconds. When she stood up and walked, there was no limp.

These were visually dramatic instant changes—by my definition definite miracles. There are more miracles going on around us than we can count, if we but knew. Who hasn't heard an instance sometime in their life about a mother faced with a child being crushed by a car, who just leaned over and lifted a whole car off that child and saved its life? How much do cars weigh? A couple thousand pounds?

Miracles can be interventions that shouldn't have been possible but happened anyway, as well as dramatic sudden healings; or they can be near misses when catastrophe seemed inevitable. Did you hear the man's story after 9/11 about the way he *didn't* go to work that day, and so he lived to tell about it? I figure that was a miracle too.

Before seatbelts, when I was toddler-age and insisting on standing up beside my mother so I could look out the window of the car we were riding in, one of those miraculous near catastrophes happened to me. My mom had her arm around me, and thought that was safety enough. But the door flew open, and I fell out head first. My mom made a wild grab with one hand and caught me by an ankle. And then was so panicked she had to struggle to get the driver's attention to stop the car. I don't know how long we traveled that way, but I know I was hanging head down out the side door of a moving car. I thunked down pretty hard on the edge of the floor when my mom grabbed me, and to this day I still have a line of permanent bruising on my right thigh to show where I hit.

Then there are miracles that are more subtle—someone just happens to be in the right place at the right time, like in this following story I found online. It doesn't even matter if the story is completely true or not, I know that this kind of miracle happens all the time, and it seems to work just as it did in this story:

"Tess Buys a Miracle – True Story"

"Tess was a precocious eight year old when she heard her Mom and Dad talking about her little brother, Andrew. All she knew was that he was very sick and they were completely out of money. They were moving to an apartment complex next month because Daddy didn't have the money for the doctor's bills and our house. Only a very costly surgery could save him now and it was looking like there was no-one to loan them the money. She heard Daddy say to her tearful Mother with whispered desperation, "Only a miracle can save him now."

"Tess went to her bedroom and pulled a glass jelly jar from its hiding place in the closet. She poured all the change out on the floor and counted it carefully. Three times, even. The total had to be exactly perfect. No chance here for mistakes. Carefully placing the coins back in the jar and twisting on the cap, she slipped out the back door and made her way 6 blocks to Rexall's Drug Store with the big red Indian Chief sign above the door. She waited patiently for the pharmacist to give her some attention but he was too busy at this moment. Tess twisted her feet to make a scuffing noise. Nothing.

She cleared her throat with the most disgusting sound she could muster. No good. Finally she took a quarter from her jar and banged it on the glass counter. That did it!

"And what do you want?" the pharmacist asked in an annoyed tone of voice. "I'm talking to my brother from Chicago whom I haven't seen in ages," he said without waiting for a reply to his question.

"Well, I want to talk to you about my brother," Tess answered back in the same annoyed tone. "He's really, really sick...and I want to buy a miracle."

"I beg your pardon?" said the pharmacist.

"His name is Andrew and he has something bad growing inside his head and my Daddy says only a miracle can save him now. So how much does a miracle cost?"

"We don't sell miracles here, little girl. I'm sorry but I can't help you," the pharmacist said, softening a little.

"Listen, I have the money to pay for it. If it isn't enough, I will get the rest. Just tell me how much it costs."

The pharmacist's brother was a well-dressed man. He stooped down and asked the little girl, "What kind of a miracle does your brother need?"

"I don't know," Tess replied with her eyes welling up. "I just know he's really sick and Mommy says he needs an operation. But my Daddy can't pay for it, so I want to use my money."

"How much do you have?" asked the man from Chicago.

"One dollar and eleven cents", Tess answered barely audibly. "And it's all the money I have, but I can get some more if I need to."

"Well, what a coincidence," smiled the man. "A dollar and eleven cents—the exact price of a miracle for little brothers." He took her money in one hand and with the other hand he grasped her mitten and said "Take me to where you live. I want to see your brother and meet your parents. Let's see if I have the kind of miracle you need."

"That well-dressed man was Dr. Carlton Armstrong, a surgeon, specializing in neuro-surgery. The operation was completed without charge and it wasn't long until Andrew was home again and doing well.

"Mom and Dad were happily talking about the chain of events that had led them to this place.

"That surgery," her Mom whispered. "was a real miracle. I wonder how much it would have cost?" Tess smiled. She knew exactly how much a miracle cost... one dollar and eleven cents... plus the faith of a little child." (8)

Isn't it time to move into creative imagination and the realm of possibilities and miracles? Isn't it past time to shut up the nonstop blathering of the reproductive imagination that never stops speaking pessimistically to us? Aren't you tired of feeling "Oh, I can't go there; there are barriers. There are too many limits to what I can do."

Sometimes our walls of limitation are as flimsy as the tumbled rock walls in an ancient ruin, once intended to be barriers, but no longer effective to hold us back from getting over them. Ignore the walls— break through some old thinking patterns and enjoy the freedom of new possibilities.

"Think left and think right and think low and think high. Oh the thinks you can think up if only you try."

Dr. Seuss

Declaration #3: I have the absolute right to imagine.
Declaration #4: And I have an unlimited ability to imagine.

ೞ೮ೞ Chapter 4: Source Material for Dreams

You see things and you say "Why?"
But I dream things that never were, and I say "Why not?"
George Bernard Shaw

Instead of focusing on the things that have already happened or are happening in our lives now, on circumstances we cannot seem to change, that draw an anguished "Why?" from the depths of our being, let's turn ourselves around and start looking forward. Imagine an attractive future and start saying, "Why not? I'm going for it."

This is where it starts to get fun. Look forward to some new things that will be pleasant and enjoyable to experience, and make them the focus of our thinking. Who wouldn't rather focus on something new and good rather than the "been there-done that" things of our past? Begin thinking possibilities for a better life. Start a new habit of seeing and thinking about our possibilities more than we think about anything in our past. It becomes easier with practice.

Our repeated focus strengthens our possibilities into probabilities. This means that by focusing our attention on our new possibilities, we are increasing the quantum odds of our brain releasing neurotransmitter activity into that new thought direction rather than already existing pathways. Our brain metabolism is being changed. We're creating parts of our brain that didn't exist before our intentional focus began. (1)

> *Try this*: Set aside some time to imagine new things for yourself, for your life. Get quiet and relaxed, then picture yourself at a designated time in your future feeling entirely satisfied. Now look around the imaginary you and discover what's happening around you. What are the contributing parts to this fulfilled you? Where are you, what are you doing, who is around you, what does it look like, sound like, smell like? Apart from the satisfaction, exactly what are you feeling? Are you excited, immersed in whatever you're doing; are you content, at peace? Break it down until you have a detailed picture of what you're wanting your future to hold.

I suggest writing down new details the same day we first see them.

Describe the things we're discovering about our future selves. After our initial unhurried session, spend at least 5 quiet minutes a day in this imagining exercise. As we do, what we are envisioning for ourselves will take on clarity, detail, and it will with repetition over time become a very real place in our imagination. We won't realize it as it's happening, but one day when we visit this possible future self, we'll think with surprise "Wow; I really do believe this is going to happen to me!"

> *Imagination is everything.*
> *It is the preview of life's coming attractions.*
> Albert Einstein

We may not know what will fulfill us yet. Just the idea that what I imagine can be life-shaping is *huge*. So start small, begin by asking yourself: What do I want? Make a list. Make it a long list if you can. In Chicken Soup for the Soul, there's an account of a 17 year old young man who sat down at his kitchen table and wrote out his life's wish list, the same kind of a list I'm advocating here. The story is "Another Check Mark on the List" by John Goddard. He amassed 127 life goals, some of which are exploring 8 rivers, climbing 16 mountains, studying primitive cultures in 12 countries. At the time his story was published, he'd accomplished 108 of them. (2)

Be relentless with yourself about looking for possibilities. Become your own imagination police—you enforce the forward-directed, possibility thinking. Refuse to spend your thought-time looking backwards: picture a locked door every time you stop a broken-record-memory that would replay itself over and over without your deliberate interruption. Picture yourself taping a snapshot of the new possibility you're picturing for your future on that locked door.

Make this determination: I will pursue new things; I will imagine new things for my life. Break through some limitations, some of your "same old, same old" habitual thinking and imagine something new! Just make a start. The harder it is to do, the more we can be sure we need it.

Declaration #5: I will imagine new things for my life.

ᎴᎾ Chapter 5: The Doors of Opportunity

We've seen that the challenge with our imaginations is to keep our reproductive imagination from interpreting our present options in the light of how our circumstances and experiences have played out in the past, regurgitating scenes from memory, and predicting that our future will be just like what we're remembering. We've lived in that vicious cycle long enough.

We need to yank our imaginations out of the loops of memory whenever we find ourselves remembering, remembering. We need to *think possibilities*. We need to unleash our creative imagination to shuffle the possibilities around, even if they look familiar. We are looking for new solutions, and aiming for new goals, not a repeat of past experiences.

The third element of dreaming

The third element of dreaming is Choice. To choose means to pick the one you want out of multiple options, to select from a number of possibilities, to pick by preference.

This part of the process is dependent on a lively hope enabling us to imagine new possibilities. It's only logical that the more we imagine possibilities, the more potential choices will be available to us. Given our unlimited capacity to imagine, the possibilities before us are endless, and this directly equates to an equal number of potential choices.

It's probably a new thought that we have unlimited choices, isn't it? We've allowed ourselves to feel helpless, thinking we don't have any other choices than to try to survive the life we're in.

We are the source of our own opportunities

When one of the possibilities we've imagined resonates with our hope, and we choose to explore it, then it becomes a potential door of opportunity. We become the source of our own opportunities. We are limited in this only by ourselves, either by not taking the *time* to build our hope and imagine possibilities, or by defaulting to the inner "I can't" reasoning we've lived with so long without trying to change it.

I am where I am today because of choices I have made. (1)

We all are where we are in life because of choices we ourselves have made. The most extreme example I can think of to illustrate this is the story of a friend of mine, G.D., who got involved in prostitution as a teenager, and so immersed herself in the lifestyle that within a few years she became a Madame. As she tells it, she was an extremely angry young woman, and this life did not provide enough outlets for her anger. She decided to invite a demon into her life so she could have more power with which to express her anger. She deliberately did it and then spent years being a prisoner herself, instead of having control over the power she'd wanted. She says there is still a blank period of years in her memories, spanning the time from the very day the demon came until the day she "woke up" and got her life back (by prayer and intervention on the part of her family). She spent years in a very bad place as the direct result of her own choices.

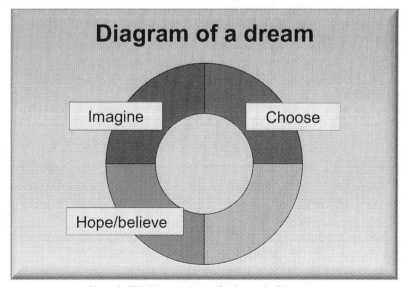

Chart 5: Third component of a dream is Choose.

What's missing today in our lives is not really what life has thrown at us, or anyone has done to us. We are all living the results of our own choices: whatever it is that influenced our choices of the past, or what our experience has taught us to expect that makes it seem like history keeps repeating itself, or what we think we deserve out of our faulty "personal truth." The good news is that we are not locked-in to these things for the rest of our lives.

We can change our choices.

We don't have to stay in the messy places to which our past choices have brought us. We can change our choices from *anywhere*, at *any time*. This is scientific fact: we have all the abilities necessary for considered decisions regardless of our circumstances. We have self-awareness, imagination, conscience, independent will, an extensive memory bank of information, and a central core of values—all the subconscious abilities that work in conjunction with our heart to give us the ability to *choose* how we will react in any situation. (2)

We said earlier that it's necessary to this process of dreaming to examine our hearts for this reason: the heart is at the core of our subconscious mind, and it acts like a command center—what issues out of this central core affects every part of our lives. Our hope, our reality, our truth and our identity are all located here. All the capacities that make us able to function as human beings are affected by and take "must-be-obeyed" orders from our heart.

The heart and the brain have different priorities, as well as different functions. Science is exploring a root idea that "energetically, the brain revolves around the heart, not the other way around." (3) We have underrated the role of the heart's mind in our perceptions of how the subconscious mind works.

If we set ourselves to make new choices and dream a new dream without examining what is already in our hearts, we may find ourselves unable to carry out our new choices. The heart has its own agenda—and the heart always has the "last word" in what we do. It is difficult to pin down and know straight out what that agenda is as the heart doesn't rationalize in the same way as our conscious brains do. The heart has the ability to misrepresent itself and it circumvents our conscious decisions all the time, in order to stay true to its personal truth code.

Balance originates in the heart, not the brain. It is the heart's job to keep us centered on our life truth, to keep us healthy and "sane" by causing our life to be lived within the confines of that defined life truth and identity. Our health in general starts with our heart attitudes and beliefs. "A sound heart is life to the body." (4) I'm sure you can see the danger in having faulty "truth" in your belief systems and leaving it unchanged—it could impact your very life.

I was discussing this concept with a young lady recently, and explaining that the things in the heart aren't readily accessible for us to know and understand, but it's vital to find out what the heart's truth is, because the heart reaches out and pulls our new expectations back into line with its truth standard. And she gave me a perfect example of how it works: She was waiting for a phone call from a young man that interested her, and he was hours later in calling than she had anticipated. And her emotions skyrocketed. The conclusion her heart made was that "it wasn't going to work out, because it never works out" and that's exactly what she said, with tears. Her heart was trying to give her perspective and protect her in a dangerously emotional moment by pulling her expectations back into a familiar and therefore "safe" place of disappointment.

> *Inside yourself or outside, you never have to change what you see, only the way you see it.*
> Thaddeus Golas

What makes this heart process difficult to understand is that heart's truth doesn't have to be true; it can be and more often than not is a twisted conglomerate of deep-set conclusions, gathered over time and not all consciously known to us. And in protecting our equilibrium according to that truth standard, our heart hands down a less-than-satisfying decision that we *will live out*. What we think is good will not always match what our heart decides. But like I said, the heart has the final say in what we will do.

The problem is not your problems; it's how you look at them.

What we put in or give room to in our heart contributes to and shapes what we believe, what we expect and what we do. The belief system, the personalized truth, and the unique identity that reside in our deepest heart affect all parts of our life and are stronger than our best, most intense conscious decisions. So let's continue to practice making paradigm shifts in our imaginations so we can look at the possibilities of life rather than the difficulties we see or our past failures, in order to make different and better choices for ourselves from an increasingly bigger pool of possibilities.

But let's also learn to know and get in tune with our hearts so we're no longer working at odds with the part of our heart system which has the final word on what our futures will hold.

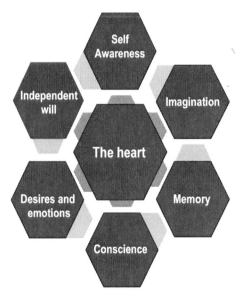

Chart 6: The Subconscious Mind

Our amazing subconscious mind, we noted, is constructed like a central motivation center from which all its other mental functions receive their orders, much like a king issuing decrees from his throne in the center of our subconscious mind's activities. The subconscious functions we are concerned with for the purpose of developing our dreaming ability, all of which are subject to the heart's dictates, are self-awareness, imagination, independent will, memory, conscience and desires and feelings. These all have a part in our choices.

Self-awareness

Self-awareness is a uniquely human trait; it gives us the ability to mentally step outside our circumstances and evaluate our options, without the suffocating effect of our emotions. Self-awareness is the ability to see how what is happening is going to affect me, and to decide how I will respond to it, to choose how I will react in any situation.

> *Try this exercise to experience how it works:*
> Close your eyes. Picture yourself standing leaning on the wall of the room you're in, looking at yourself where you are sitting with your eyes closed. This is self-awareness.

Self-awareness gives our imagination the ability to step outside current circumstances and picture ourselves in different possibilities, in order to try them out and make choices apart from the pressures and emotions of the present moment. The best example I have ever heard or read of how self-awareness works is found in the following passage from <u>The 7 Habits of Highly Effective People</u> by Stephen R. Covey:

"Let me share with you the catalytic story of Viktor Frankl. Frankl was a determinist raised in the tradition of Freudian psychology, which postulates that whatever happens to you as a child shapes your character and personality and basically governs your whole life. The limits and parameters of your life are set, and, basically, you can't do much about it.

"Frankl was also a psychiatrist and a Jew. He was imprisoned in the death camps of Nazi Germany, where he experienced things that were so repugnant to our sense of decency that we shudder to even repeat them.

"His parents, his brother, and his wife died in the camps or were sent to the gas ovens. Except for his sister, his entire family perished.

Frankl himself suffered torture and innumerable indignities, never knowing from one moment to the next if his path would lead to the ovens or if he would be among the "saved" who would remove the bodies or shovel out the ashes of those so fated.

"One day, naked and alone in a small room, he began to become aware of what he later called "the last of the human freedoms"—the freedom his Nazi captors could not take away. They could control his entire environment, they could do what they wanted to his body, but Viktor Frankl himself was a self-aware being who could look as an observer at his very involvement. His basic identity was intact. *He could decide within himself how all of this was going to affect him.* Between what happened to him, or the stimulus, and his response to it, was his freedom or power to choose that response.

"In the midst of his experiences, Frankl would project himself into different circumstances, such as lecturing to his students after his release from the death camps. He would describe himself in the classroom, in his mind's eye, and give his students the lessons he was learning during his very torture.

"Through a series of such disciplines—mental, emotional, and moral, principally using memory and imagination—he exercised his small, embryonic freedom until it grew larger and larger, until he had more freedom than his Nazi captors. They had more *liberty*, more options to choose from in their environment; but he had more *freedom*, more internal power to exercise his options. He became an inspiration to those around him, even to some of the guards. He helped others find meaning in their suffering and dignity in their prison existence.

"In the midst of the most degrading circumstances imaginable, Frankl used the human endowment of self-awareness to discover a fundamental principle about the nature of man: *between stimulus and response, man has the freedom to choose.*" (5)

I don't know how self-awareness could be illustrated more clearly than that. Dr. Frankl's example leaves us no room to argue "but my emotions are too strong for me" or "my circumstances are just too horrendous. We *can* evaluate and make choices apart from both our emotions and our circumstances.

Memory

We have a conscious mind memory, and a subconscious memory. From our conscious mind's memory bank we can pull a limited number of available items at will, like recent events, things you've just learned or memorized, etc. With time however, unless we are using the memories frequently, all memories are archived into our subconscious memory, to leave the conscious mind's short term and working memory capacities free to deal with the present, the recent past and information coming from the world around us through our five senses. All the rest of what we know and remember is stored in the subconscious mind.

The subconscious memory is like a vast mental library holding every bit of information our mind has gathered since we were born, but we cannot freely access just anything at any time. We pretty much have to put an order in for a certain memory like we were requesting a book from a mental librarian, and then wait until it shows up at "Will-Call", which would equate to our conscious memory. If what we're trying to remember was part of a traumatic moment in our past, our memories may be "stuck" under excessive subconsciously-stored emotion, and the heart may attempt to block our remembering, trying to maintain our balance and equilibrium. Remembering some things therefore may be a lengthy process.

Imagination

Imagination is the ability to create in our minds, to see what hasn't been part of our experience before. It's what lifts us above living by whatever circumstances come our way, simply reacting to things we didn't start. Imagination supplies possibilities for our choices, and draws from an either forward or backward direction.

Creative imagination is the ability to take items from our memory bank of experience and observation and form new combinations of possibilities from known or familiar things. The creative imagination looks forward; it is all about new possibilities. Every bit of our creative imagination is another potential window of opportunity.

Reproductive imagination is imagination looking backwards; it gathers instances of our strongly emotional memories and concludes that things happening in the present will have a similar result to those events in our past experience. It works like a prophetic disaster reflex, virtually calling similar bad situational outcomes to repeat over and over again in our lives. There's no new possibility thinking in our reproductive imagination.

Conscience

Conscience is that part of our belief system that evaluates our choices and tells us whether we've made a good or bad choice, and how good or bad it was; like a teacher marking test scores on each choice we make. Conscience doesn't shout, it just quietly evaluates what we're doing according to our moral scale, and we hear it in our quiet moments. My conscience still tends to sound like my mother at times, although she has been gone over 20 years.

Conscience is a deep inner awareness of right and wrong, of the principles that govern our behavior, and a sense of the degree to which our thoughts and actions are in harmony with them. We define "the good life" as living with a good conscience.

Independent will

Our independent will is the ability to act based on our self-awareness, free of all other influences. (6) It is the center of our ability to choose, to make judgments. The ability to choose is at the core of what makes human beings special, the capacity that enables us to rise above animal instincts as we go about our day-to-day lives. We can live by deliberate choices, rather than merely responding to circumstances as they come our way.

Emotions

The ebb and flow of our emotions have been compared with the restless waves of the seas. Our emotions have high points and low points; strongly visible dramatic moments and deceptively calm moments. Emotions are constantly in motion, and they can be all over the place. If we live simply according to what feels good to us at the moment, we too will be all over the place.

Our emotions have a far more important role than we have credited to them, though. We have more or less thought of our emotions as naughty children; any time they're left on their own to play, they go too far and get in trouble. Recent science has proven that emotions are informational molecules tied to and holding our memories in place in our subconscious minds, on a cellular level all throughout our bodies. "Repressed traumas caused by overwhelming emotion can be stored in a body part, thereafter affecting our ability to feel that part or even move it." (7) The traumas in organs or body parts held in place by too much emotion can be harbingers of health problems on the way, if not already manifesting in our bodies and/or in our minds.

Emotions are meant to be all positive, all expressed and released, not hoarded. Bad things happen when too much emotion gets "stuck" somewhere in our body/minds. Excess emotion holds our trauma "signposts" in place, so the memories remain a painful focus in us. As they keep growing in size they increase in the ability to affect our health and our future.

Heart's throne

The most central part of our subconscious is where our personal wisdom and strongest motivations originate. It's the command center of our whole lives—physically, emotionally, in our relationships, and in our deepest mind places. It's like an internal throne room with an absolute ruler on the throne. Whatever we have decided to be the thing or person who can satisfy us is what (or who) sits on our heart's throne, and every part of our life is affected by that decision. Whatever or whoever we look to for our satisfaction is essentially the god and king of our lives and will influence every decision we make; every intention and plan we come up with will be centered around that thing, concept, or person.

Make your own choices

Looking back at our lives, if we're honest with ourselves, we can see how our choices have landed us where we are today. Our choices determine our actions. Choices govern our lives. If I want to make changes in my life, I have to make different choices.

People with little hope will not imagine many new possibilities, nor will they make good choices out of the possibilities they do see. They more often than not default on their choices, letting someone else or fate make the choices for them, or repeating the choices of *choices* the past. The problem with defaulting is that no one else is as motivated as I am to choose for my best interests; everyone else is working on their own priorities. And even though I have not made the actual choices, it's exactly like handing someone my credit card or my car keys—I will pay the consequences of any decisions that are made. Not a happy scenario.

> *"Everything can be taken from a man but one thing: The last of his freedoms—to choose one's attitude in any given set of circumstances, to choose one's own way."* (8)

If we don't make our own choices, we have essentially already made the choice to let others make our choices for us. If that's you, how has that been working for you?

We can make choices ourselves, or continue to give our choices to people and circumstances and try to survive whatever comes. We can spend our whole lives putting out the fires of one crisis after another resulting from our defaulted choices, or we can choose to intentionally sow hope and build some new dreams.

A strong hope is integral to good choices being made out of an active imagination engaged in creative possibility-thinking. Our imagination supplies possibilities to our self-awareness, and our independent will coupled with our emotions enables us to pick what we want, and make that one thing our choice. The more possibilities we come up with, the more potential choices we will have, and there's no ceiling limitation. The possibilities are endless. That is quite a concept—when we consider that not one iota of circumstance or situation has to change first for this process to be wildly successful. It's all in our amazing subconscious minds—in every single one of us, without exception.

Choices vs. intentions

Mental choices are merely intentions until we put action to them. Intentions can sit around and gather dust for years. Don't they say that the road to hell is *paved* with good intentions? So choices, to be valid and life-changing, require corresponding actions.

Choose to begin taking action toward your best life. Reading this book is an action. Doing the exercises as you read through is effective action. Even thinking about and coming to a fuller understanding of what you want is action.

Deliberate dreaming is an action.

Choosing to dream is an action that can change our lives from the inside out. As our thinking begins to focus on our dreams and we continue to make the choices our dreams require, our actions will change. We'll find ourselves headed in the direction of our best life, with some progress already made, and all we will have done is choose, think and speak a few things out loud.

Make this choice today: I am not giving away my power of choice any more. I CAN step out in new choices based on new possibilities.

Declaration #6: I have the absolute right to choose.

ೞೞ Chapter 6: Effective Imagination

Now that choice has joined imagination and hope in the dreaming process can you see how it's starting to come together?

> *The capacity for hope is the most significant fact of life.*
> *It provides human beings with a sense of*
> *destination and the energy to get started.*
>
> Norman Cousins

Our hope may be just starting to live again, and it may still be tiny and seem fragile, but it is an anchor that ties us to the fulfillment of our dreams. There are many things we can do to increase the strength and size of our hope. One of the most effective is the dreaming process. Beginning to imagine new possibilities around our hope, putting *time* into our imagining, is one of the best things we can do towards changing our life.

Make a list of possibilities as they occur to you. Keep a journal that you can carry around with you. Take it with you wherever you go, and keep it within reach at all times. The flexing of our imagination is precious, and we don't want to lose a speck of new thinking.

Start contemplating possibilities as potential opportunities. Give your creative imagination new rooms of thought to explore—picture yourself actually doing each of the possibilities you've got on your list. Ask yourself: How does this activity make me feel—is it satisfying and enjoyable? Does doing this make me feel happy and fulfilled?

> *The first step to doing great things is not to do, but to see.*

Since the first real step to doing great things is not what you do, but what you see, evaluate what you're doing for its effectiveness, and ask: Is there more to this than I have seen and imagined yet? What can I add to it?

When you have explored all the potential doors of opportunities as best as you can, choose the one that stands out as your favorite, and start a more intensive imagining focus on that one. Think about it before you go to bed at night and right when you wake up in the morning. Keep making notes. Hone this opportunity before you put action to it, by mentally examining it in mind's eye from every side. What will it look like fully operational? In 5 years? The more we can dream this, imagining it in detail, the more sure our action steps will feel, and the more confidence we will have even in the beginning of our actual doing.

If our first action steps show us that there are flaws, details we didn't or couldn't foresee, write out what we did, what we need to do now, what we need to think about for future dreaming and planning. It's all good. It's all part of the process of living out of our creative imagination, and it makes life an adventure.

Hope, imagination and choice are our inalienable rights. They are capacities deeply programmed into our make-up as human beings. As long as we live, we can always have hope and build it stronger; our ability to imagine has no limits; and we get to choose how we will react to everything. These are absolute truths that no one can take away from any of us.

Hope is free. Imagination is free. Choices are free. Where else on earth can you get so incredibly much accomplished for free?

Declaration #7: I choose to see myself living in my dreams.

ೞೞ Chapter 7: Speaking as effective action

When we get a mental picture of what we want, and hope tells us it's possible for us, we begin to imagine the possibilities around it, and make new choices, then we're well on the way to what we want before we've even lifted a finger in physical activity. How good is that?!

The fourth element of dreaming

Finally we come to the fourth and final component in dreaming, which is to deliberately SPEAK and anticipate what we speak with FEELING. The reason this fourth step works and makes dreaming a successful process is that our words are *extremely* powerful. The Bible says that death and life are in the power of the tongue, and that we eat whatever we say. (1) I have heard it put this way: "We will live tomorrow in the things that we say today." It made the hair stand up on the back of my neck when I first realized it, as at the time I was saying things like "this job is killing me" and "this is an impossible work load." I'm here to tell you that I stopped saying my job was killing me *immediately*.

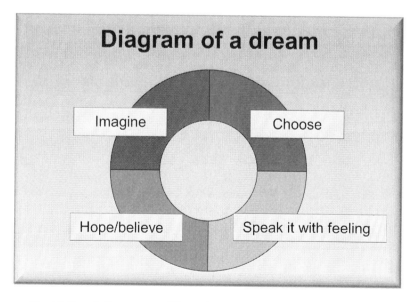

Chart 7: Fourth Component of Dreaming is Speak it out loud with feeling

Our own words are the greatest power we have. Science has discovered a place in our brains that is activated *only* by our own verbally spoken words and our whole physiology opens up to receive those spoken words.

> *Your own words are the bricks and mortar*
> *of the dreams you want to realize.*
> *Your words are the greatest power you have.*
>
> Sonia Croquette

What we say, we hear. What we hear, we are programmed to believe. What we believe, we live by, and it ultimately comes to define us. "Your words and thoughts strengthen synaptic connections in your brain, changing your neural patterns, or networks, giving you a personal experience of reality and potentially bringing about the results you want. Spoken words—either positive or negative—have the power to create a reality you either want or don't." (2)

Know our real starting point

Most if not all of us have an idealized idea of where we are in life. To move into our best life, we must have a clear picture of our starting point. If I want to step into a new place, I can't step from "over there," I have to step from right here where I actually am.

Let's look at the phenomenon of speaking and believing in two ways: first discovering what's already in our hearts by listening to what we say, and watching what we do, like it was a TV show or movie, in order to understand what I already believe. Every time I do this exercise, I learn something about myself. My own words are a true indicator and a reflection of what's in my heart. There often seems to be a rude shock reaction to what I discover, but it gives me a new baseline understanding of where I really am.

And then I can start *from that point* speaking differently. We need to pay attention to these things in ourselves. It's certain that others do. Ask someone who knows you well to tell you how you speak about yourself and your future. This is not an exercise for the faint of heart. We're likely to hear the unvarnished truth. We're usually more comfortable ignoring a few things about ourselves, and thinking we're okay even when we are broadcasting "not okay" by what we say and do.

> *The only limits to the possibilities in your life tomorrow are the buts you use today.*
>
> Les Brown

Every time we say "but" we are speaking a limitation into being. Make a commitment to yourself to stay on this issue until you have mastered speaking positively.

When we look into the mirror of our own words and actions, we can see what's hidden in our own hearts. The Bible says "Out of the fulness or abundance of the heart, the mouth speaks," (3) and "Keep your heart with all diligence, because it affects everything you do." (4) What's in our hearts *will* come out of our mouths, and show in our actions, as surely as the sun comes up every morning.

Just recently a friend was asking me why an acquaintance continually pointed out the controlling, manipulative actions in everyone around her—and I reminded her of the Bible verse I just quoted above. What this woman was being irritated with in everyone around her, and commenting on, was really her own unaddressed heart issue. That's a third way to know what's in our own hearts, besides our words and actions—what do we see everyone around us doing? It's probably not their big problem, it's ours, if we're seeing the same problem cropping up all over the place around us.

What we say matters

It's not what happens to us that ultimately harms us, it's what we tell ourselves about it over and over that does the real damage. Initially some of us will take exception to this statement, because of the horrendous trauma and pain we've lived through, which truly did harm us. That past trauma is *still speaking* in painful echoes through a deposit of stuck emotions in our cells; however, now it's being reinforced within us by our own words. We hold painful memories in place ourselves by what we ourselves say, verbally or internally.

One man I know had only several older sisters. He learned to read at a slower pace than his sisters, and because of it, he heard "you're slow" way too many times as he grew up. He equated slow to stupid, believed it, and all during school had to struggle to pass his classes. As an adult, he found he could figure out how to fix or build just about anything, and he became a skilled handyman. The intelligence was there, but the label came out even in adulthood, when he'd be the first to say to himself "that was a dumb move," really meaning "I'm stupid."

The subconscious mind recognizes our internal focus, based on the repeated, emotional thoughts and words we feel and say and the memory pictures we associate with them. And our "signpost" focuses continue to grow bigger with each repetition so that whatever the pain is, we will feel and live it again. And again. And again.

Second, begin to talk like we're already living in our dream.

In order to complete the dream process, we need to spend thought-time projecting ourselves forward into our dreams, as if they were already accomplished, and we were already in the middle of that place, activity, relationship, position. This requires two things besides a little of our time: mental visualization and emotional involvement in what we visualize.

Then we must speak into our present reality *from that future place.* We are able do this because we have the ability to experience what we don't technically have yet. Our self-awareness gives us ability to visualize things so clearly in the windows of our imagination that we can *feel what it's like* to be living in our dream before we actually get there.

When we see it and feel it, then and only then do we create the declarations we will speak every day to pull our dreams to us.

We need to rephrase our dreams into "I am living in" statements. The best format I have found for making declarations that work comes from <u>Chicken Soup for the Soul: Living Your Dreams</u> (5) (*Chart is on page 76*). I have taken minor liberties in shortening it, while retaining the integrity of the information.

Speak it out

We make declarations out loud with the same feeling we felt in mentally projecting ourselves into our fulfilled dream (no matter how we feel right now). Jump around if you have to—your subconscious mind will not be able to tell if you are faking the emotion. It cannot tell the difference between a faked enthusiasm and real joy. Whatever we repeatedly say with strong feeling, visualizing it and holding the image in our conscious thoughts, our subconscious mind takes *as a command.* (6)

Only frequent repetition of strongly emotional statements can drive our new directives into the cells of our subconscious mind, and plant living seed deeply where it can germinate and grow into life-transforming new truth in our belief system. The good news is that when we do this, it affects every cell of our body—sicknesses can be reversed, stresses dropped off, our immune system is strengthened, and the body itself reflects positive changes as our subconscious mind begins to embrace the corrected beliefs we are seeing and declaring.

The only thing that will stop you from fulfilling your dreams is you.
Tom Bradley

Tap into your future feelings, so whenever you state your dream out loud, you *rehearse the feeling* that goes along with the dream. Vigorously!! Reach for your dreams with both hands. Make your dream declarations as often as you think of them during the day and particularly first thing in the morning and the last at night. Force yourself to put some "yahoo/yippee" emotion into them when you say your declarations. It's important. The emotion is what drives your declaration deeply into your cells, but it doesn't have to be heart-*felt* emotion to be effective. In other words, faking it works.

Watch your words

From now on, be careful of your words. Never again discount what you're saying as a little thing and not significant: a world of change is contained in each declaration you make. You are speaking life into a place that didn't exist until you started speaking it. The Bible says: "Death and life are in the power of the tongue." (7) We have the ability to speak life and we have the ability to speak death. Be careful not to un-declare what you've just declared by speaking doubt or negativity. Our doubtful, negative words are just as creative as our dream declarations because they have emotions with them too, don't they—fear, anger, the uncertainty of doubt, etc.?

Let's put our life-and-death word power to good use in creating what will truly satisfy and fulfill us. Our verbal declarations frequently repeated with strong emotion are unstoppable; they drive the new information of our dreams into the subconscious mind, and can literally make something live that never existed before.

This dream process we're beginning to implement in our lives is physically creating a new room in our brain, a new capacity to be filled with new skills, new thoughts. Science is calling this ability of our brain neuroplasticity. Like plastic, which can change its form, and then hold its new form permanently—as opposed to "elastic" in which the new form would revert to the original once the forces that changed it were removed—our new dream visualizations can change the material structure of our brain. "One reason we can change our brains simply by imagining is that, from a neuroscientific point of view, imagining an act and doing it are not as different as they sound. When people close their eyes and visualize a simple object, such as the letter *a*, the primary visual cortex lights up, just as it would if the subjects were actually looking at the letter *a*. Brain scans show that in action and imagination many of the same parts of the brain are activated. That is why visualizing can improve performance." (8) The brain is plastic and physically changes its state and structure as we think, in ways that can be tracked by electronic measurements. (9) What good news for us! The dreaming process is scientifically provable! We can think our way into our best life!

The good news is that you don't know how great you can be!
How much you can love!
What you can accomplish! And what your potential is!

Anne Frank

Dream on

Dreaming is a circular process. We jump in, and begin working each part, but we don't *have to* start in only one place. We can start with an imagined possibility, or a new choice, but all four elements are essential to successful dreaming. We must have hope; it's our bottom line requirement for dreaming a new dream. It's the emotion that motivates us to look forward with the awareness that this is possible for *me*. It works with our imagination; as we begin to imagine possibilities, our hope will speak up like the chorus line "yes, yes, we can do that." Hope keeps telling us "this is do-able" as we make specific choices out of the possibilities we've imagined. Because of that seed confidence, we can move into the next step and begin to visualize and speak what we're dreaming, in order to speed up its coming to pass in our lives.

Dreaming is also cyclical. Each step impacts the other elements and enables them to stretch out a little further into our probable future. The dreams we begin to dream will spiral around and grow bigger as we work the process. As we listen to our own dream declarations, we hear ourselves and believe what we hear. And then our hope becomes stronger yet for even more imagined possibilities, and therefore more potential new choices, which we reinforce by declaring them out loud with enthusiasm, and so on, and so on. And we will be changing dramatically all the while, enlarging our own intelligence and our brain's ability to accomplish our dreams without having lifted a finger against adverse circumstances!! The statement "Anything is possible" is more true than we have ever credited. The sky *is* the limit for the diligent dreamer.

Declaration #8: I am visualizing and speaking my dream to speed up its coming.

Writing Goal Declarations That Work

1. Start with "I am."

Whatever you say after "I am" your subconscious mind takes as an order, and begins working to make happen. Whatever you say "I am," is not only a description, but is actually a prescription for the future.

2. State it only in the positive.

Tell it what you want rather than what you don't want. Avoid using the word "not" because the subconscious mind deletes this negative word as it takes in the rest of the command.

Wrong: I am not afraid of job interviews.
Right: I am calmly answering every question in my job interviews.

3. State it in the present tense, as if it's happening now.

By stating it as if it's happening now, you create "structural tension" in your subconscious, and if you repeat your declaration often enough, it *requires* your subconscious mind to figure out how to make it come true in order to relieve the tension.

4. Keep it short and easy to remember.

Apparently the subconscious also likes rhyme and cleverness. If your ideal weight is 175: "I am feeling alive at 175!"

5. Make it specific.

Wrong: I am driving a new car.
Right: I am driving a 2004 crystal-white Lexus LS430.

6. Include an action verb ending in "-ing."

I am *driving* a 2004 crystal-white Lexus LS430.

7. Use a feeling word in it.

I am *happily* driving my new 2004 crystal-white Lexus LS430.

8. Make it about yourself.

Wrong: I am happily watching my teenager clean up his room
Right: I am enjoying lounging in my well-cleaned and orderly house.

Chicken Soup for the Soul: Living Your Dreams (5)

Section Two:
What Got in the Way of Our Dreaming?

Knowing how the dreaming process works since we've looked at all four parts is not all of the journey into our best life; we need to look at what has kept us from dreaming and living that best life up until now.

ೞೞ Chapter 8: Dreamstealers

We all started out with dreams.

We all start our lives believing anything is possible. Creative imagination runs rampant in children, working effortlessly. Children draw freely from their creativity, and believe completely in the wonders they imagine.

Childlike Faith

When we were children, there was no hesitation in acting like we already were whatever we were pretending to be. We believed we could do it and be it, and we talked it, and acted it out every chance we got, we felt it and lived in it. It didn't matter at all how preposterous the pretend was. Impossible or possible was not even a factor. We walked around totally believing we were firemen, doctors, astronauts, dragon slayers, etc. and acting totally in character without any self-consciousness at all. We ran, jumped and wrestled full out, making up the rules of play as we went, and underneath it all, learning about ourselves and the world.

The world was once endlessly fascinating. Remember? Everything was once all new to us, there to be explored and discovered. We were curious about everything in our world, and we started out fearless. We *expected* life to be fun. Children are prepared to enjoy themselves, and without even thinking about it, they always have an expectation that fun may be about to happen at any moment. Just ask a child to play—their eyes light up and you've instantly got their full attention.

Imaginative playing

Playing and play-acting are such a natural part of childhood. Do you remember what you loved to play when you were a child? I loved exploring in my grandma's deliciously intriguing and somewhat spooky attic the summer I was seven when we went to visit her in Ohio. To this day I can picture the dust motes floating in the sunbeams that shone through the window at the end of the attic onto the wooden plank floor, and I can almost smell it.

There were wonderfully unfamiliar things to find everywhere—a record player you turned a handle to make play, a bookcase full of *very* old books, a wood-strapped leather trunk full of old clothes. My sister and I loved to play dress up and pretend we lived in another century. The attic was from another century, so it lent itself to our play-acting. It's a strong memory.

What games did you play when you were little? The first six years of my life, my family lived in a tiny village in Alaska with no roads, or TV, or much access to anywhere else in the world except through radio and telephone. Our home town had a mile-long boardwalk along the beach from one end of town to the other. I didn't know such a thing as television existed until we moved to Seattle when I was seven.

Perhaps because of this isolation, our childhood play was very inventive and imaginative, and our toys were simple. My sister and I made elaborate houses in the woods by our house, and cooked dirt pies. I kept trying to talk her into tasting them. We played tag with other kids, jumping around on the logjam on the beach. We looked for treasures when the tide went out, and played hide and seek under the boardwalk. I even remember getting in trouble one time for climbing up and trying to walk along the handrails of the boardwalk, like they were a tightrope. If I'd fallen off it would have hurt—there were devil's club and pushki (a native plant) growing right up to the edge of the boardwalk. The one has wickedly long thorns and the other could have given me a nasty rash.

All of these things held within them clues to things that I would choose to do as an adult. I never had any difficulty entertaining myself, and ideas came easily to my mind as a child. As an adult, I have started multiple businesses, and I paint and do other creative artsy things. Where I loved to explore and play on the beach and look for treasures as a child, today I tend to be a bit of a risk-taker, and I'm not afraid to try things I've never done before. I look everywhere for value, and expect to enjoy wherever I find myself. I take roads on purpose to see what's down the road a ways, hoping to get where I need to ultimately be by way of places I've never seen, and something about exploring the unknown still draws me.

Pretend games

One of the pretend games children play is "What I want to be when I grow up." The reason all children pretend is because it's a God-given ability: it's a function of our self-awareness, acting in sync with our creative imagination.

This ability is built into all of us. My friend Tina is from London, and tells of walking home from school every day with her brother. They would pass by the "sweetie shop" (candy store), and would invariably tell each other that when they grew up they would own it, that very shop, so they could eat as much of their favorite sweeties as they wanted. Did they grow up to own that shop? No, but today they are both entrepreneurial, and involved in multiple business ventures. Their playacting together showed the gift behind their fledgling entrepreneurial dreams flexing its wings for the first time.

Think back to your childhood—what were your childhood dreams? What did you want to be when you grew up? See if you can recapture how you played, what you pretended to be, and examine it for the beginnings of abilities or heart's desires that remain in your life as an adult.

Because God put it there, the ability to play and pretend you are someone else, or somewhere other than where you literally are is still there. You haven't lost it, even if you haven't used it for decades. It has never been removed, although it may be dormant, buried under disappointments and life's detritus and it may require some digging to get to it. But I promise you, it's still there. Imagining you are already living in something you don't have yet is an important part of dreaming, and an ability we would all do well to cultivate in our lives. It's another of your absolute rights as a human being.

Start using this part of you again. *Pretend* you have a strong "I CAN" to do and be whatever you want, like we all had in childhood: What is your wildest dream? How big can you imagine? Let your imagination run with this, and see what you come up with.

Lost dreams

The first time I taught this material, one dear lady looked up at me from the back of the classroom in all seriousness and said, "What if you didn't have *any* childhood dreams?" She said that because when we did an in-class exercise to remember our earliest childhood pretend-to-be, she drew a complete blank. If that applies to you also, I have to say emphatically that it is *never* too late to reclaim what you should have had and circumstances beyond your control took from you. There is a very strong reassurance in the Bible for this: "And I will restore to you the years that the locust has eaten, the cankerworm, and the caterpillar, and the palmerworm." (1) These are all growth stages of the locust. Swarms of locusts can consume every green living bit from a field and leave only bare dry ground behind them. In other words, there may be complete devastation, but it can all be restored to you.

> *Try this:* If money and time were not an issue—i.e. if I had WAY more than enough of both—what would I do? Where would I go? Who would I find a way to meet?

We should, however, look at what can take our childhood dreams from us, so we'll know where to start looking for lost dreams. Although most of us start our lives dreaming and projecting ourselves into our imagined places and roles effortlessly, there are many things that happen which either shut down our dreaming or hurt our ability to sustain our dreams.

Even as children we can see what's not right in our world, and we watch it intently, not realizing fully how it will affect us. There are people who say and do things which act like water on the fires of our youthful enthusiasms. We call these people dreamstealers.

Dreamstealers have a devastating effect on our confidence levels. By what they say to us, dreamstealers set limitations into our lives, ceilings to our aspirations. These limitations begin to act like a damper on our imaginations and they restrict our ability to see ourselves successful in our future. They program an "I can't" into our minds that is very pervasive and very difficult to expunge.

Most, if not all of us have encountered dreamstealers. Maybe we still have dreamstealers in our lives, making it difficult for us to dream a new dream. It may be necessary to re-evaluate the friends we hold to ourselves, to dig into past memories to unearth our buried dreams, and to understand what caused those dreams to be lost so we can guard against losing them again.

Who or what affects our dreaming ability? It can be the negative things that were said to us by someone we looked up to, a sibling or a parent, which undermined our self-confidence. It can be awful things that happened to us, that we were powerless to stop happening. It can be traumatic experiences where it took all our attention to deal with the after-effects of a life-calamity. It can be limitations that were put on us by the examples people set for us; labels we didn't even realize were there, let alone how much they were affecting our ability to dream and live successful lives.

Life can be lived more fully if people simply quit pretending to be who they were told to be, and be who they really are...
                                                              Doug Firebaugh

The mother who says, "Now you know I love you honey, and I just don't want to see you getting hurt by failing..." is subtly stealing her child's confidence to even *try*. She's setting up an expectation of failure. Well-meaning people can steal dreams just as easily as outright mean and spiteful people.

Every time a dream-stealer speaks into our life, disappointment and hurt follows after hearing their words. These words have a cumulative effect within our subconscious minds. And when a person hears negative things repeatedly, there's a progression of effect: from hearing some version of "you can't" and believing it to the end result of using that same rule on ourselves and locking ourselves into permanent limitations.

Hear limiting, negative things enough, and we stop having a mental "no, that's not right" when we hear them—we start accepting and believing them without question. We begin to say to ourselves "it *must* be true" and we also begin to take *ownership* of those things and feel that it's our fault somehow that this is happening to us. Sound familiar?

The next step in the process is that we start using the same limitation on ourselves without any outside input, in order to avoid more hurt and disappointment. Ultimately we find ourselves in uncomfortably tight, restricted places out of which we can no longer see any escape. It's not necessary to have a dreamstealer speaking into our life anymore at this point. By our own self-talk we keep the dreamstealer limitations firmly set in place in our lives.

Today it may be that we don't even remember we ever had dreams, or what they might have been. Or it may be that when we see a great opportunity, we think "that's for someone else; it's too late for me. I just have to make the best of the hand I was dealt." We might not be able to pinpoint where it comes from but something about where we've been makes us instantly rule ourselves out of good things that are about to happen.

These are all instances of mindsets which indicate dreamstealer activity sometime in the past. If you have limited thinking when you're trying to see your future, if you have any kind of an "I can't" going on in you making it next to impossible to imagine possibilities and work the dreaming process, you've had dream-killers in your life, just as surely as when you see little piles of sawdust by your wood walls and you know you've got bug-problems. You don't see the actual cause of the problem, all you see are the symptoms of limitations making their homes in the structure of your life.

It may be that our own actions have contributed to our losing our dreams. Remember my friend G.D.'s story of choosing to lay everything on the line for a potential supernatural power to hurt and "pay back" those who had hurt her. She had no ability to dream a new dream during her lost years. Yet she is finally living out her childhood dream. She told me that when she was grade-school age, she wanted to go to Africa. Today she is in Nairobi, Kenya, and for the past few years, she has been rescuing throw-away children from the streets, giving them a safe home, security, food, clothing, and schooling. And all the love of her incredible heart.

Where there have been dreamstealers at work, there are lost dreams. I know this was true for me. I had to start from "What dream, what passion; what are you *talking* about?"

I had to admit to myself I had no idea which capabilities in me innately pointed to my life purpose. I was not passionate about any one purpose, and I certainly was not living my life to the max. That's humbling for a forty-something year old person to admit, but it was a starting point for reclaiming my dreams.

"Whatever you aspire to do, there will always be people who tell you you can't do it; you're not good enough; it will never happen. What I've learned is that some of them are right, most of them are wrong, and all of them need to sit down and shut up." (2)

What has been "smooshed" in your heart? How has your family or life inadvertently or deliberately squelched something good in you, especially when you were little and defenseless? Doesn't the unfairness of those limitations laid into your life without your permission get your goat? Make a determination to recover the life that you should be living, without dreamstealer activity in it.

The dreamstealer process

We talked about how disappointments and delays deplete our hope. They leave us discouraged and even more susceptible to believing the misconceptions and outright lies of dreamstealers. Once we buy into self-limiting beliefs, and start repeating the negative labels that either we or someone else has spoken onto us, we start talking it and making it spiral into worse and worse places of increasingly limiting beliefs. It's not what happens to us that ultimately harms us the most, it's what we tell ourselves on an ongoing basis that does the real damage. By our own words we effectively lock ourselves into a state of dissatisfaction.

The truly awful part of it is that limitations we have believed work their way down into our identity: we feel ashamed of *being* limited.

Shame has octopus tentacles that pull down our possibility-thinking with the belief that "I am defective, and therefore I don't deserve this good thing." It acts like an insidious computer virus, and infiltrates our whole system. We find ourselves acting out a defective lifestyle and self-sabotaging any success that might begin to happen for us. We won't even allow ourselves to want what we really want because we can't see a way for it to happen. We've become our own jailers.

Reality glasses

Once we believe something on this level, even if it began as a dream-stealer's wrong limitation, it becomes part of our "REALITY"—our life truth—and no one else ever has to do anything to keep that limitation on us. We do it ourselves in spades. We repeat that lie in our own hearts like there's nothing we can do but accept it unconditionally. It no longer matters whether it's literally true or not, it is true for us, and we see everything about our life filtered through that tainted reality frame—we completely accept it as solid-as-concrete truth. It's like wearing a pair of glasses with a prescription made just for me, so that I see everything according to that personally-applied prescription for reality. No wonder our life-view is off-kilter, and we don't make the best life choices!

Do not live all your life with the labels other people have put on you and which you, rightly or wrongly, have believed. Or one day the dark clouds of despair may have all but covered any bright hopes you still hold for your tomorrows.

It has to be said—if you have dreamstealers in your life today, ask yourself, Can I live without this person in my life? Or if I can't, then how can I minimize the negativity of this person? It takes 11 positive statements to override ONE negative statement.

How long can you keep being 11 times more positive than the negativity that is coming at you? How many times was something laid on you as you were growing up that you take for granted as part of your life today? What will it take to override *that*? You may have to do some shuffling of relationships. Put positive value back into yourself, and look around you for people who will believe in your dream with you. Start cultivating those relationships.

Reclaiming lost dreams

This is very important. Remember the rule for hope: If I'm still breathing, it's my right to have hope? In the same way, it is my right to dream. Use your absolute right to choose, and *choose* to reclaim your dreams. No one can keep you from choosing to dream.

> *Here's an exercise to help.* Begin recovering lost dreams by making a life map of your key emotionally-charged experiences. This will give you a starting-point understanding of where life has brought you and where you are *right now*, and what contributed to your being here. Draw a straight line horizontally across a blank page of paper—this will be a chart of your life from birth to today. Begin marking along the timeline the points at which significant events took place in your life. *See Chart 8 for an example.*

I've laid out a five-point recovery process for reclaiming lost dreams. First of all, choosing to reclaim our dreams means changing gears, determining to use our memories in new ways; to begin pulling new plans out of our creative imaginations. It means refusing to allow either our memories or the visualizations of fear to play out over and over in our mind's eye without our protesting and interrupting the broken-record replays of emotional memories. Stop tolerating memory re-runs.

Second, it means beginning to search out the clues from our childhood dreams. We have the ability to view the memories that come up in our minds dispassionately—without emotional pain—so that we can examine them for bits that might be part of our heartfelt desires and dreams. Self-awareness gives us the ability to step outside ourselves and look at our own lives like we were watching a movie on television. Practice this, particularly if there are painful memories blocking your view of your childhood dreams.

Third, we must determine we will *pay attention* to our thoughts, and whenever our child-self peeks out—when something about a fleeting thought resonates within us that it is coming from way back in our life—write it down right away. We learn what we need from our past a little bit at a time. Be patient with yourself. It took years to bury your dreams, allow yourself whatever time it takes to recover them.

Fourth, determine to pay more attention to the "harmless" memories

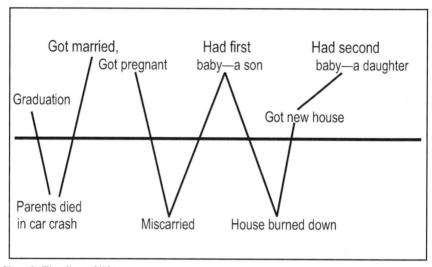

Chart 8: Timeline of life events

that float up into our conscious minds. Carefully examine them—consider the thoughts of our own minds like going on a treasure hunt. Always be looking for some clue to what's buried out of sight. The smallest memory could be the key which will unlock some long-lost remnant of a dream.

And last but maybe most important, ask God to help you reclaim the joy of discovery. You had it as a small child; we all did. We might as well enjoy the process of reclaiming our dreams, right?

Give yourself some time to rediscover your childhood dreams, and to discover your unclaimed adult dreams. And don't be discouraged by a small start. Everything starts as seed and grows. It's a universal law. By plowing the ground of our thought patterns, our emotional response habits, and the usual boundaries within which we make our choices, we are making room for the seeds of new dreams and new hope to grow. Isn't it time to unlock a few memory doors and recover some lost dreams? Isn't it time to start dreaming again?

Declaration #9: I choose to reclaim my dreams.

ೞಜಜ Chapter 9: My Faulty Reality

What are the components that make up the prescription of our "reality glasses?" The elements that can put flaws into our reality are truth *as I see it*, which may not necessarily be as it truly is. My truth doesn't have to really be truth; my misunderstandings can seem just as true to me. Depending on what else is in my reality, misunderstandings can seem more true to me than real truth.

We've talked through the progression by which wrong labels put on us by other people work their way down into our core beliefs and become real "truth" to us. Even outright lies when we have believed them can become part of our truth. I used to know a young woman named Nora who was stunningly beautiful, tall, willowy and graceful with thick blond hair that hung straight down nearly to her waist. You would think someone so gorgeous that she turned heads everywhere she went would have self-confidence to spare, but it just wasn't so. She and her sister had been verbally abused by their father when they were young, over a period of years, and instead of instilling the self confidence that fathers are able to impart to their daughters, he obviously was viciously cruel and probably told them in so many words that they didn't matter, because that's what my friend believed about herself. She had about as poor a self-image as anyone I have ever met. It wasn't real truth that she lived by; it was the misinformation of her "reality."

To lies we've believed, add our life-observations and judgments and conclusions, all definitely contaminated by the "less-than-truth" we believe, but through which we're observing and judging and concluding. Add to this mess all that we have ever done with the resulting consequences and aftereffects of what we did and it's obvious this prescription is way off base and not even close to the "true or actual state of a matter" the dictionary defines as truth. There is no consistent conformity with fact or reality, and our messed up truth won't have an actual existence anywhere except in our own deep-set belief system. It's not honest, reliable, or provably accurate to anyone else. (1)

We view and evaluate every part of life through this messed-up filter. It's already so wrong that just changing what we *do* will not be enough to set our lives right. We have to make changes in what we believe on a very deep level, in the core belief system of our reality. We have to correct our prescription for truth and get a new pair of reality glasses.

Changing my reality

The process of changing reality is very deliberate. We create *structural tension* on purpose.

A structure is an entity that is undivided, total and complete in itself—a pen, a ball, a tree, a house. A tree doesn't move all that much; it stands rooted in one place and responds to its environment by swaying in the wind. If it's a deciduous tree, it sheds its leaves every fall, and grows new ones every spring. If it's a maple tree, it doesn't grow apples. The living tree's activity and behavior are consistent throughout its life. Once a tree, always a tree. It will never move against its own nature or turn into something un-treelike; a tree does what a tree does.

Your life is a structure, and as with all structures, it will have certain ways it will act, behave and work. (2) Our life structures are many and varied with one constant: we all act according to our internal programming, which includes the teaching and molding of our environment shaping our potentials. The family dynamics we're used to are part this programming. The "way we always are" is for some of us friendly, or shy, or outgoing, or self-absorbed. Whatever is "normal" to us determines what we will do in different situations and how we will act.

If we want to know the ways the structure of our life works and why we are how we are, we ask our heart. Get into a calm, meditative place where you can listen to what your heart has to say in its gentle, quiet voice.

When we are asking the heart why it's doing what it's doing, I strongly suggest keeping a journal. Write the question you've asked, and then write in the snippets that make themselves known as they occur to you. The heart must answer us as to what's in it, but it won't come all at once.

Our past experiences which still have so much feeling tied to them are emotional markers, and our subconscious heart bases our "norm" in a large part on those highly-charged emotional moments, good and bad. We talked about how the subconscious mind doesn't sort between good or bad, truth or fantasy, etc. However, the subconscious mind *does* recognize focus, and it works at making our emotional focuses repeat themselves in our lives. Because they're the familiar, the known, the "normal" that we've been used to, we let those memories repeat themselves in our minds uninterrupted, where with each repetition, they are gaining intensity.

The beginning of interrupting that repetitive cycle is to use our self-awareness, that absolute right and ability to stand apart from our pain and consider our life objectively, and look at what is in the motivation center of our life-structure, the heart. We examine dispassionately the memories and the focuses we find there: Is this memory okay to leave alone or is this a cycle I should consider interrupting and changing?

Any emotionally charged image or idea that is repeatedly held in your conscious mind is processed as a command by your subconscious mind. (3)

Once we've identified a piece of our flawed reality that needs to be changed, we make a positive declaration to override and change it. State the good we'd rather have as if we were already experiencing it. (*Refer back to Chapter 7 for the formula to make declarations.*)

Repeat that declaration out loud every day with feeling!

Remembering that the subconscious mind cannot recognize real or not-real emotion, and that the addition of some whooping emotion is what makes your repeated statement a *focus* to be reproduced, feel free to "fake it until you make it." Structural tension is then created in the subconscious mind by the discrepancy between our spoken statement and our current reality. This tension will not be allowed to remain. "A basic principle found throughout nature is this: Tension seeks resolution. From the spider web to the human body, from the formation of the galaxies to the shifts of continents, from the swing of pendulums to the movement of wind-up toys, tension-resolution systems are in play." (4)

The subconscious mind begins to work overtime to resolve the tension by making our statement a reality, thereby overriding the flawed bit and moving us into the positive place we've been declaring repeatedly and enthusiastically, not feeling it yet but hoping we're right and this process is working.

Knowing that the subconscious mind recognizes our repeated emotional declarations of corrected truth as a focus to be reproduced in our life means we can consciously choose to put things into our subconscious that will change our reality. It's so important to take some control back from the reservoir of not-truth has been fed into our belief systems without our permission. This opens up realms of possibilities, doesn't it?

In summary:

This is the key. It's very simple, really.

1. It requires a statement you make up with your conscious mind, deliberately, and say *out loud*.

2. It requires you to fake some strong positive emotion. Try a whoop of a shout, a Yeah!!

3. It requires repetition. So don't quit!

As we learn what's really going on in our hearts, in our subconscious minds, and become aware that our truth is a little shaky, we have the ability by this simple process to change beliefs that are so far out of our reach otherwise that we'd be taking them to the grave with us, unchanged. This is huge.

Try this: Pick just one thing to change, make a declaration that will override it with new corrected truth and repeat it with strong emotion every day for 30 days, and then take stock of how things have changed, and decide at that point whether or not to make more changes.

Declaration #10: I can change my reality.

෴ Chapter 10: Dealing With Loss and Pain

Dealing with Loss and Pain

> *For there is hope of a tree, if it be cut down, that it will sprout*
> *again, and that the tender branch thereof will not cease.*
> *Though the root thereof wax old in the earth, and the stock*
> *thereof die in the ground; yet through the scent of water*
> *it will bud, and bring forth boughs like a plant.* (1)

As long as we live, we can rebuild hope and start new dreams. But how do we deal with the pain we're still feeling from our past experiences? The opportunities we've lost, the people we once loved who are no longer in our lives, the activities we truly enjoyed that are no longer possible for us, the dreams we've set aside to deal with the practicalities of life—these are only a few of the myriad emotional losses life can bring us. Our response to losses of all kinds is grief and sorrow. There is a lot of unresolved grief in our lives.

If we try to ignore the pain of loss, we may or may not be able to function. But until we finish the grieving process, we will stay emotionally chained to the painful event, and it will keep us from moving forward into our best life.

If we try to just tough it out and go on about our life, we're virtually living with an emotional volcano inside us. It may appear dormant, but when we start stirring up our subconscious for dream clues, whatever we have avoided grieving can suddenly flare up right in our face, feeling like the event that triggered it just happened even though years may have passed. We need to heal from our losses.

In January of 1992, my mother died unexpectedly, leaving my father living alone, but unable to fully care for himself, as he'd had a stroke a year prior to her death. I dropped everything to go take care of my dad, and ended up spending four years of fairly intensive, 24/7 time being with and taking care of him. It took so much of my energy to juggle my job, Papa's needs and his emotional well-being that I put off grieving for my Mama during those four years. When my father died in 1996, I found myself double-grieving. With all the most altruistic reasons for putting off grieving, it came back on me anyway and my mother's death hit me hard when my father died. I felt the loss of my mother like it had just happened, on top of the loss of my father and I could barely function.

At that point I had to give up all hope of doing anything else *but* working out the grieving process for awhile, until the sorrow abated. There was a lot more that contributed to my feelings of pain and loss at that time of my life than I feel would contribute to my point here by listing it all out. Suffice it to say that when I look back on this spring and summer of my life, the picture that comes up is me sitting curled in near-fetal-position in the corner of the sofa with a book and the TV on—for weeks.

Grief is an intensely private process. "The heart knows its own bitterness and a stranger does not share its joy." (2) Grief is defined as keen mental suffering or distress over pain or loss; sharp sorrow, painful regret.

However, grieving is a positive, healing process. It is typically broken into either five or seven separate steps. The process is not linear; that is, the emotions of grief do not follow a one-after-the-other pattern in us. The whole time we are grieving our emotions are jumping around from one extreme to the other and all the places in between. They run together, overlap and occur without explaining themselves. We can and do experience any and all of the steps repeatedly, and bounce around from one to the other as long as the grief process lasts.

Scottish proverb: *Were it not for hope the heart would break.*

Grieving isn't a fast process, nor can we gauge how long it will take us by how long we saw it take in someone else's life. It is different for everyone and there is no pre-set right or wrong length of time. It takes as long as it takes. Just hold onto your hope as you go through the grieving process, knowing that eventually you will be done. It is a *process*, with both a beginning and an end.

The stages of grief

The first stage of grief is shock and disbelief. This is not a bad thing—that numb feeling of disbelief acts as a buffer zone which keeps us from being overwhelmed all at once. When my mother died, I went "home" and slept in my childhood room, in a familiar bed. What I remember particularly is how at first waking I was hit with the most severe shock and disorientation I'd ever felt. The world without my mother was not one I expected to have to face for at least another 15-20 years (she was 67), and I was not prepared. I wanted to be comforted being in my mother's house, with the morning sunshine coming in the window onto the foot of the bed, but every part of me was internally screaming "NO!"

The second stage is denial. Our world is shaken by our loss, and on some level, denying the reality of our loss is sheer pain avoidance. I guess the whole internal "NO" was the beginning of this stage, although the shock and disbelief had not worn off at all. I kept thinking there must have been some mistake, until talking to my father, and he said when he found my mother, in the morning after she'd died, that there was no question that she was dead. I didn't ask for details. I didn't want to know. I wanted then to think of my mother as alive, and see her that way. Part of that was undoubtedly trying to avoid the thought of her loss, denying its finality.

The third stage is bargaining. This is a futile effort to find a way out of the pain and despair, to trade something to remove the loss: "I will be extremely good for the rest of my life. Please let my loved one recover." I didn't have a chance to work this stage, because my mother's death was so unexpected. I did some proficient bargaining though during the four years I spent with my father. The doctor's prognosis when my father had his stroke, my mother had told me, was for two more years. After she died, that left him a year by my estimation. I'm pretty sure I promised everything I could think of to God for more time with my Papa than one year. I didn't realize then it was part of grieving, but I'm very grateful for the four years he had with me, instead of just the one I expected. Maybe because his going was expected, I was pre-grieving? That may explain why my mother's sudden death seemed to hit me so much harder.

The fourth stage is guilt: feelings of remorse over things we did or didn't do when we had the opportunity. This can be a crushing load. This part was hard. I still feel remorse for not showing love to my mother more in the little ways she liked—mushy cards in the mail for no reason, little baskets I would find here or there to add to her collection, finding little places nearby to "explore" with just her. We were all so focused on my dad, being 11 years older than my mother and already having had a stroke. We missed the clues, and maybe shortchanged my mother, in paying more attention to my father. I try to pay attention to the people around me now, and show appreciation. I don't want to be caught off-guard like that ever again.

The fifth stage is anger, in many variations of intensity, from frustration to rage. When frustration gives way to anger, we may lash out and lay the blame for our loss on someone or something else. I *was* angry. Sixty-seven was too young, and we still had things to do together. I felt cheated and it made me mad. The frustration part came because there was no one around me to whom I could talk and with whom I could sort it out. It might have been easier on me to yell at somebody, but I'm sure it wouldn't have been a fun time for that somebody.

The sixth stage is depression, but not the pressing funk that weighs a person down for no discernible reason. This can be a part of the healing process; coupled with reflection and loneliness, it's a time of processing our loss. This was the latter part of my fetal-position-in-the-corner-of-the-couch season. I definitely isolated myself, self-medicating myself with murder mysteries and sentimental movies, but little by little memories inserted themselves into the in-between moments. I started to remember, and my Mama-memories are mostly good ones. Just remembering was therapeutic, even though it hurt. Grieving definitely wrings you out. I cried until I had no more tears, yet for months, it took only the tiniest things to reduce me to tears again.

The last stage is acceptance and hope. Out of the reflection time will come a time of working out new ways to cope with our life, and a time of looking forward again. (3) My new way to cope with life without my parents is to pay more attention to the moments I am in and who's here in them with me. To celebrate the people I love whenever I think of them by visit or letter (email), or small gift—I believe my emphasis on this behavior can be traced to the aftermath of grieving for my parents. I have a new enjoyment of people, and I place a higher value on time spent with the people I love than I used to in my earlier years. I don't take the people in my life for granted.

The danger of getting stuck

The danger in grieving is that some of the emotions we experience in this positive process have a negative connotation to us most of the time—depression for instance. If we don't let the process proceed, if we hold to the depression and "get into" being depressed, we won't finish the process naturally. Other non-helpful and definitely negative emotions will move in alongside the depression. We can get overwhelmed and what began as part of a positive process could morph into a permanent negative place that works its way down into our identity until it is integrated into the beliefs that define us.

Example: Despair and self-pity can come from unresolved grief. There is a pulling power to these emotions, and you *don't* want to go there, ever—picture yourself being caught in a huge whirlpool and sucked underwater. There is a woman I know who was widowed when her sons were very young. She got stuck somewhere in the grieving process long ago, because when I met her it had been many years since her husband died. Both her sons are fully grown, yet her demeanor is still one of "poor me" and barely being able to cope. She lives like a mole, hiding in her darkened house, and barely showing up in the light of day to go buy groceries. And when she does surface, she sucks all the sympathy out of the room just by showing up. More than twenty years after her loss, it's still very draining to be around her.

Take time to finish grieving.

The grieving process works itself outward like the pattern of a spiral: there is an epicenter from which you go around and around, but slowly move farther away from the center. Think of the pattern of a spider web, with a central point from which it spirals farther out with each circumference. So it is with the emotions of grieving—they are intense and all-consuming to begin with, but each time around, there is more breathing space between the grief-emotions re-occurring and to a degree in the intensity of the emotions themselves.

Weeping may endure for a night but joy comes in the morning. (4)

Follow through on the grieving process, and look forward to being eventually done with the process. Don't try to bypass it, and don't stop yourself in the middle of it. Don't listen to anyone who says "Oh, get over it already," by outright words or by insinuation. Give yourself permission to fully experience it, and for the process to work itself out naturally in your life. Finish grieving and move on into your morning, and into your best life.

Forgiveness turns out to be much more about you
than about the one who has hurt you.
Barbara Cawthorne Crafton

The key to healing cleanly from our grief

While we are in the grieving process, there are things we can and must do to move ourselves into a healthier place, into the territory of new hope and positive life changes. The most crucial thing we must do is *forgive*.

Forgive whoever hurt you, not for their sake, and not because they have in any way earned your forgiveness. Forgive them for your own heart health. Unforgiveness is too damaging to us to hold onto it. Never mind what unfairness happened, forgive yourself for taking part; for being in the wrong place; for not being smart enough to avoid it; for allowing the wrong to happen. Even if we were powerless to stop it, we may still be carrying around a feeling of responsibility. Forgive yourself, so you give yourself a clean slate for a fresh start, and for reclaiming territory to grow new good things in your life.

How to forgive.

According to the dictionary, to forgive means to cancel a debt, or an obligation—that person no longer owes me for what he did. It means to grant pardon to a person, to give up all claim to revenge. These actions don't have to wait for healed feelings; they are choices.

Forgiveness begins with a choice. We begin to forgive by deciding to forgive, *not by feeling like forgiving*. This is an extremely good thing—if we had to wait until we felt like it, there would not be much forgiving going on in the world. To forgive also means to cease to feel resentment against—this is the fulness of forgiveness, the end result of our beginning choice to forgive. This will come with the passing of time.

To forgive is to set a prisoner free and discover that the prisoner was you.
Lewis B Smedes

There is a definite release that comes with forgiving. It is true that when we forgive, we experience a measure of freedom. When I choose to forgive, I stop giving my emotions permission to focus on that person or event and feel resentment. Resentment is little brother to bitterness. And bitterness kills something in the one who harbors it. Being bitter doesn't hurt the one who offended me—it hurts me. I cannot afford to let any resentment breed bitterness in my life. The other person involved in my painful event can go on forever without being sorry or changing, but I must be set free of a severe negative focus that eats at me. Unforgiveness is dangerous—even if you do everything else right, harboring unforgiveness can kill you.

Choose to forgive

Decide to forgive. Make a specific choice to forgive. Remember, we have the absolute right to choose, and the choice can be real even if it goes against our emotional inclinations. Choose it over and over again until it eventually *feels* real. This is another place where our self-awareness will make that which is necessary possible.

You make the choice, but ask God to make it real in you, to work the process out in your heart and bring the emotional healing. This is how I did it—I said "I choose to forgive. God, please make it real in me," every time an offense came into my mind. I said it for the same offenses over and over (they were ugly) but eventually they stopped coming into my mind. I can't tell you how many hundreds of times I had to choose and choose again, before it finally became real as far as my *feelings* could tell. Where once I couldn't even think of that episode in my life without crying, now I can relate the details of the whole nasty experience from beginning to end without a twinge of emotion. This process works. I am living proof.

If we want to short-circuit any future wrongs from taking up bitter, resentful residence in our heart (and for that read anywhere in our whole "bodymind"), try creating a habit of forgiveness. Practice forgiveness on the little things whenever we can. You may think this is humorous, but I practice forgiving people as I drive. The freeway especially provides *lots* of occasions. I do a lot of forgiving that way. It's gotten easier.

Be afraid to hold grudges. The Bible says that if we don't forgive, we won't be forgiven by God. (5) Whether we fully believe that or not, let's err on the side of caution, and not hold grudges. The new science says forgiveness is the trigger that releases the excessive emotions holding your painful memories trapped in place in your cells, like time bombs of future disease. Practice forgiveness, for your own sake.

In summary, recognize where and what you're grieving, and work through it. Don't try to stuff your grief down and ignore it, hoping it will go away. And don't get hung up in the middle—finish the process. Choose to forgive. Just like morning surely comes after the longest night, grieving will end with a new day for you. Your best life is still ahead of you.

Declaration #11: I will grieve what I need to, and finish the grieving process.
Declaration #12: I choose to forgive, for my own sake.

Section Three:
A Fresh Perspective

Now that we know how the dreaming process works, and where our disconnects with our dreams stem from, we need to re-examine ourselves, our lives, our hearts and to begin to rebuild our lost dreams and dream a new dream.

෪෩ Chapter 11: A Fresh Perspective of Who I Am

What lies behind us, and what lies before us,
are small matters compared to what lies within us.

Oliver W. Holmes

There is only one You.

There is more to each of us than we have realized; none of us have known ourselves as we really are. There is a vast potential for greatness in every living human being—the capacities are built into us. And every one of us is unique. If uncountable snowflakes can be individual and unique, how much more human beings?

"Whenever two people meet there are really six people present. There is each man as he sees himself, each man as the other person sees him, and each man as he really is." (1) Too often we form our image of ourselves based on what we think other people think of us, or a compilation of what we have heard people say about or to us, rather than who we are in truth.

To be nobody but yourself in a world that is doing its best
to make you just like everybody else means to fight
the greatest battle there is to fight and to never stop fighting.

e.e. cummings

Just being oneself is not easy. I found a charming poster offered online one day that said "Confidence: It's not who you are that holds you back, it's who you think you are." It's our own opinion of ourselves that really matters.

> *Try this:* Make some lists about yourself: What comes naturally to me? What are the good things I know about myself? What am I like?

Personality defined

What is personality? The dictionary says it is the visible aspect of one's character as it impresses others; it's the essential character of a person. Psychology says it's the sum total of the physical, mental, emotional, and social characteristics of an individual. Personality is the organized pattern of behavioral characteristics of the individual. (2) It's what defines your character and what makes you act like you do. It's what makes you uniquely you.

Where does our personality come from? We know it is part of that central heart place, that complex and intriguing subconscious part of us from which all our life emanates. But what makes up our personality and our identity?

> *I am bigger than where I am.*
> Elinor Alexander-Southcott

We said that our core belief system holds our personal truth, our reality. Is part of that reality responsible for our personality and our identity? All of what we think does and does not define us can be based on wrong reality, wrong personal "truth" laid into our hearts, and this makes a personality re-discovery necessary.

What does NOT define us.

Our circumstances do not define who we are. Circumstances and life situations are just the boot-camp exercises we have to get through to become the best us we can be.

Our experiences and our past do not define us. What I have lived through is merely history. History does not have the ability to tell me who I am, unless I make it a signpost focus.

Our environment, our family, our society, our culture—these are just the game-board on which our lives are conducted. Where I live, who my family is, this is not the essence of me. These things explain some of my *learned behavior*, but again, they don't tell me who I am or set the boundaries of my potential.

One lady named Leticia shared with me that her mother had told her all her life she was a mistake and that she was almost aborted. That unspeakably harsh statement certainly colored her life. It could have held her captive in a toxic place her whole life. It might even have completely annihilated her, but Leticia now lives on purpose, and she has a warmly influential life. You would not know her background held such cruelty unless she told you. That part of her history no longer defines who she is.

The same holds true for our income level, our education, or lack of education—these may be good or bad factors in our life, but they don't tell us who we are. Didn't Abraham Lincoln go quite a long way without a formal education?

Our race and our appearance, along with what people say we are able to be—these are no impediment to dreaming an impossible dream, or to becoming a giant among men. They tend to be excuses for not pushing to be all we can be more than anything else, rationalitics the "I can't" in us uses to justify not trying.

There is more in us than we know. If we can be made to see it perhaps for the rest of our lives we will be unwilling to settle for less.
Kurt Hahn

If we look at reality spread out like a map, there are only two sets of reality maps that are possible for us to have. There is the way we think things are, the "reality" we see out of our flawed subjective perception, and there is the way things really are, the ungarnished objective truth. There is my reality, and there is actual reality. I doubt if there is a person walking on the earth who lives fully in objective actual reality. We all have our own individualized truth.

Finding who we are takes some sorting out, then. Most of what defines us is in our subconscious; like computer programming, it's invisible but necessary for our lives to function properly.

What really makes up our personality?

We looked at the chart of our subconscious mind, with the capacities of self-awareness, memory, imagination, conscience, will, desires and emotions—all revolving around a central core, the heart.

107

Now let's examine what is in the heart itself, the composites of different information that determine who we are. I've divided heart's core into four parts: our deep-set sense of self-worth, our source of direction, our motivation, and our reality. These make up the control center of our life. These comprise the Rule Book of our heart's judgment criteria: the value we put on ourselves, the direction we've chosen to take in our life and what motivates us to head in that direction, all woven into and viewed through the filter of what we believe is true.

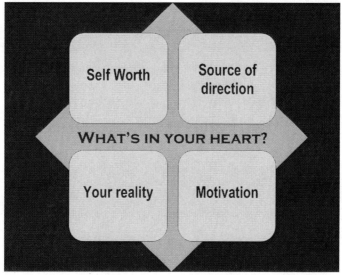

Chart 9: What's in your heart?

Self Worth

Our self-worth is our self-image. It's who we believe we are and how much we value ourselves. Our sense of our own worth, our identity as seen from our own eyes, acts like our emotional anchor. The subconscious mind keeps us in a place of being true to our self-esteem, whether that's a healthy place for us or not. The heart can and does effectively sabotage our every break-out success, pulling us back to ensure that we stay in alignment with our low self-esteem. As Eleanor Roosevelt said "No one can make you feel inferior without your consent."

It's interesting, though; what defines us in our own eyes is also visible *on* us from the outside. It's like having the labels we have absorbed into our identity and taken as our own printed on the outside of our skin. If for instance we've been victimized, we often go around with an aura of "victim" on us that draws the very thing to us we most vehemently want to avoid.

One woman I met is the widow of an extremely abusive man. She is still withdrawing and shy to the point of apologetic in manner. It used to be real work to hold a conversation with her, because she didn't seem to be comfortable talking. She almost cringed with the need to be invisible. Even though her husband has been gone for several years now, the damaging effects of that abusive relationship still show on her life. The terrible beating her self-confidence took for years instilled a low self-esteem identity that was very visible. The moral of the story here is that what we think of ourselves *shows*.

Source of direction

Our source of direction is a key factor in the choices we make. It's our purpose; it keeps us oriented toward a goal that serves to guide and motivate us. It's where we've determined our life is going and what we live for.

Take for example those who have determined to be famous. It colors every decision they make, right? Or think how single-mindedly some people pursue money, or some people pursue being in just the right relationship. How many life choices are guided by these and similar motivations, things we have focused on as being the one goal that will satisfy us, that thing or person we set our hope in. If in the beginning it was a choice, now it has become our guiding focus and our life's direction.

Motivation

Our motivation is what gives us the energy to make choices, and what gets us moving to act on our choices. It's our capacity to act on our decisions. We can have a life focus without the motivation to get to it. There used to be a gag gift available, and maybe there still is, that was a circular flat object with TUIT written on it. Motivation is our "round-to-it."

At one point a few years ago, my brother was in a hard place financially, and appealed to me for ideas and help. I worked up a business idea, for which I funded the materials, and he was to begin doing some furniture refinishing, which I would then help him to market. He had the skills in spades to begin a highly successful new career that he would truly enjoy, and which he could do right out of his own garage—but he never even started it. He remained focused on what he saw lacking in his life and it seemed to suck all the "round-to-it" right out of him.

I think motivation is tied to our hope, because motivation is what makes the difference between pipe dreams and real dreams. We have to believe a thing is possible for us before we are able to differentiate between pie-in-the-sky unrealistic wishes and real hopes. Then it's like hope is the wagon, and motivation is the driver, and together they are able to move our dream choices into the action of confident reality.

Our Reality at work

We've talked about our reality as being our prescription for "reality glasses," the filter of our individualized truth through which we view all of life. I've broken this reality into parts also. Our personalized reality-filter provides our perspective, our sense of balance and it colors all our judgments.

Our perspective is our understanding of the world *as it relates to me*, as seen through and determined by our flawed reality. My world view always has me in the center, and my perspective is how I see the world around me through the filter of my reality glasses. I make sense of what I see this way and determine within myself how I should react to what's happening.

Our personal sense of judgment is our understanding of how all the parts of life *relate to each other* and how principles apply to it all.

When we see something happening, and our reaction is "That's not fair!" it's our sense of judgment speaking. It's our moral viewpoint. Some of us have strong senses of justice, and of what is right and wrong. Others of us don't understand what the rules are, and we don't always know what is right or wrong. This is very personal; it is part of how we sort out what we are seeing through our own reality glasses. It's not likely to exactly match anyone else's viewpoint.

Our sense of balance is our discernment, our understanding of *how we fit into* what's happening around us. It's that part of us that tells us how much to get involved in what's happening. It's how we determine what's required of us in any given situation.

A healthy heart is the basis of a balanced life. Being in tune with our heart allows harmony between our emotions, our thoughts, our physical bodies and keeps our stress levels down. If we have a healthy heart, it will have a positive focus and expect good things. We will have a personal reality-glasses prescription that doesn't deviate too drastically from actual truth, enabling us to have better judgment and a more enjoyable life. We know only too well by experience how easily screwy concepts can sneak in and be incorporated into the heart, and from there move out to influence our whole lives. The Bible says "Above all else, guard your heart, for it affects everything you do." (3)

The visible heart

If we haven't done it yet, how do we discover, at this point in our lives, what's in our hearts? One of the ways our heart is visible to us and to the world around us, is by our personality. Personality is defined as the visible aspect of one's character (*heart*) as it impresses others. It's the organized pattern of behavior the world sees, the essential character of a person, dictated by and originating from what's in the heart.

Psychology says personality is the sum total of the physical, mental, emotional, and social characteristics of an individual. However, if the heart is working with a flawed truth imprint, ask yourself, isn't my personality going to be adversely affected? Maybe my present personality is no more the total real me than my reality glasses are the perfect prescription of truth? How much freer and happier would I be more fully in sync with my real personality?

Our personality is known by our actions. I'm going to point you to several personality tests, none of them original to me, all found online. Try one or try all, but take some time to find a fresh perspective on your own identity as the world experiences it, that is, that which is in your heart acting out through your personality.

Personality Test #1 http://smalley.cc/free-personality-test

Personality Test #2 http://www.41q.com/

Personality Test #3 There are four main personality types, and four subcategories to each, per the Jung-Myers-Briggs personality types, with D. Kiersey descriptions of each personality type. Find their free test online at: **http://www.humanmetrics.com/cgi-win/JTypes2.asp**.

Personality Test #4 One of these tests told me: "You are responsive to challenges in a practical, realistic and enthusiastic manner. You are a fact-oriented person capable of providing help based on solid information. You are assertive, self-sufficient and individualistic. People are likely to perceive you as being rational and creative at the same time." **http://www.123test.com/disc-personality-test/**

Personality Test #5 http://www.123test.com/disc-personality-test/

Personality Test #6 http://www.yourpersonality.net

> *Be a first rate version of yourself,*
> *not a second rate version of someone else.*
> Judy Garland

When you find your identity, get comfortable with yourself, and be the best YOU that you can be.

In a very real way, you choose what colors your life. In other words, your identity is who you say you are *in your subconscious mind and heart.* If you want to make lasting positive changes, you must make them on a heart-deep level in your subconscious mind, for your changes to "stick."

Hurricane Ridge, Olympic National Park, Washington State

Get the big picture

Once we've seen the view from a mountaintop, we remember it in the back of our minds forever, wherever we go. It makes an indelible impression on us. As a child I saw this view from Hurricane Ridge in the Olympic Mountains in Washington State, where you are standing eye to eye with the mountain tops. I have loved the view and the broad perspectives seen from high places ever since.

In the same way, if we ever saw ourselves the way God sees us, we would never look at anything in the same way again. "Therefore, if anyone is in Christ, he is a new creation: old things have passed away; behold all things have become new." (4) This is a perspective that once experienced makes a lasting impression and changes how you look at the "lowlands" of everyday life for the rest of your days.

Don't settle for living in low places any more. Get the big picture.

Rebellion against your handicaps gets you nowhere.
Self-pity gets you nowhere. One must have the
adventurous daring to accept oneself as a bundle of
possibilities and undertake the most interesting
game in the world—making the most of one's best.

Harry Emerson Fosdick

Rebellion and self-pity accomplish nothing in the long run except wasting our own time. Shouldn't we rather do as the man says here, and accept ourselves as a bundle of possibilities, and start working to make the most of ourselves? Who knows, if we're not fighting with ourselves internally, we may even find we like ourselves more.

Let's get a fresh take on who we are, and learn to live in that new awareness.

Declaration #13: It's OKAY to be me.

☙☙ Chapter 12: A Fresh Perspective of My Value

In this next chapter, whether it's your personal viewpoint or not, please allow me to build on the premise that the following verse from the Bible is true, that God created everything. Track with me down this road awhile, and let me make some observations.

> *For by him were **all things** created, that are in heaven, and that are in earth, visible and invisible.* (1)

Assuming this is true, nonetheless let's leave the rest of creation and talk only for now about human beings. We are "fearfully and wonderfully made," the Bible says. (2) Science agrees that the human machine is incredibly complex and amazing. Just like there are no two people with identical DNA, in many other ways we each are unique, one of a kind. It's not only "okay to be me," it's a *good* thing. We all have a different mix of gifts and talents to bring to the world.

Although none of us have moved past the point where changes can be made as long as we're still breathing, many of us haven't arrived where we are today straight-out-of-the-box clean and innocent, unscathed by life's experiences. Our self-esteem may have taken some pretty big hits along the way. We could all use a fresh perspective of our value and a boost in our confidence levels.

> *He chose us, actually picked us out for His own, in Christ before the foundation of the world.* (3)

Not a single one of us is here by accident. Far from it: we were deliberately designed down to the tiniest detail in the imagination of God. The Bible says before the beginning of the creation of anything else, before the earth even began to be formed, God the Creator of all things thought each one of us up, in every minute aspect of our being, from our birth to the end of our lives.

My whole set of likes and dislikes; what makes me laugh; what I get excited about; what takes my breath away; the things that I love to do to the point that I forget about time passing for being so engrossed in them; how I like to spend my free time—all these things about us are intentional. God is in these places before we are, thinking about us and anticipating our reactions, enjoying us as we live the lives he's so anticipated in his thoughts about us.

We were each made with a set of abilities, heart desires, and personality traits uniquely our own, and with a good purpose and a valuable contribution to make to the earth.

From a creator's viewpoint

I want to talk to you for a moment from a creator's viewpoint. If we look at the viewpoint of a natural artist, we can maybe get a clearer picture of the Creator. I myself am an artist. I have been trying to get the perfect pictures I see in my mind out into the open through various mediums my entire life, with varying degrees of success. There are some attitudes and feelings I have as a creator about what I am making, and I'd like to list them as an analogy of how the Creator probably feels about us.

If I make something, I know how I want it to be in its end result from the first brushstroke at its beginning, and I use the right raw materials to get the job done. I don't start painting on a lump of clay, when I'm making a painting. I get paper or canvas, stretched and primed, I get the paints and brushes of the right size, color and quality that I envision I'll need to get the picture in my mind's eye out onto the canvas and give it an identity of its own.

I know the purpose of what I am making, before I even start to make it. A picture is a means of communication, and when I paint it, I'm saying something. I don't make a picture and use it for a dustpan to sweep up debris. Or take my painting and use it to cover a spot on the floor. Those would be uses I didn't envision for my painting when I made it. They could work, but would undoubtedly damage it.

Since what I make takes a certain amount of my time, and I'm putting my vision, my skill and my purpose into what I am making, by the time it's done, I know it inside and out. No one else knows or understands my creation better than I do. If I'm successful about what I'm doing, there may be "experts" in the future who feel they know what I meant by what I did, but they'll have to wait until I'm dead and gone to know what I mean better than I do.

I definitely put some of myself into my creation in the process of making it. Therefore I always feel I have a vested interest in what I've made, even if it's in someone else's possession. I almost always know where it is and who has it, or at least where it went when it passed out of my hands.

I make things for my own enjoyment. Why would I put myself into something I don't like? Occasionally I will make something that is not my most favorite thing, but its purpose gives it additional value in my eyes. While not everything ends up being my favorite, I put a personal touch on each thing I make that makes it distinctly mine. It's an expression of a part of me.

Therefore, in the future, whenever I look at what I have made, I feel an attachment, a kinship. I enjoy seeing my touch on it after it's done and remembering what I was feeling while I made it.

While I am in the middle of the creative process, I don't have a lot of tolerance for criticism. It may look like total chaos to an onlooker, but I am working to the standard of an internal vision. No one can see what I'm seeing from the beginning—you have to wait until the end and hope I get what I see out onto the canvas, before you can understand how the parts fit together and make sense.

I only make valuable things. If I didn't see value in it, I would scrap it and start over. So I take pride in what I have made. If I feel these things about what I create, how much more does the Creator feel about us?

The Potter and the clay

I've expressed the creation process from my viewpoint as a painter. Now let's look at it another way, through the analogy of a potter's work. A potter starts with a handful of raw clay, perhaps freshly dug out of the earth. He begins to work it with his hands, warming and softening it, squeezing it back and forth, hand to hand, until it is soft and malleable. This takes quite a bit of time. As he works it, he is picking out of the clay any bits of rock or dirt he finds, removing the clay's imperfections as they show up in the kneading process. Occasionally he'll take the lump of clay and *forcefully* throw it down on a table or the floor, then lean on it to smash it flat, before picking it up and continuing to work it in his hands. He has to get all the air bubbles and dirt out of the clay before he starts to form it into the vessel it will ultimately become.

This can take awhile, and so water needs to be added to the clay to get it just the right consistency and keep it there while the kneading and cleansing process continues. This process is also vital as it changes the clay on a molecular level, making it able to be formed and fired in a new shape without falling apart into its original clay-dusty bits.

Let's say this lump of clay is going to be a bowl—the next step will be putting it onto a potter's wheel, and spinning it around and around while the potter begins to poke and pull at it. It spins in the center of the wheel while the potter gradually forms it into the shape he has in mind, alternately stretching the clay and applying pressure to force it into shape. The final shape is built from the bottom up, little by little.

It's not an easy process on the lump of clay. Stretching, pulling, smashing flat and starting over if an imperfection shows up, smoothing, squeezing smaller, etc. The pummeling seems to go on forever. Not one part of the process resembles the clay's "comfort zone"—that place of rest in a bank of earth where it was found.

Even when the clay becomes a pot, a bowl, a cup or whatever, and is fully formed into the right shape, it's not finished. The fine-tuning comes next—a final smoothing, any cut-outs for design, (*eek, knives*)—and then the furnace. If the smashing and kneading in the first step was not done thoroughly enough, when it goes into the furnace, no matter how much time and care may have gone into the forming of it, the heat will cause air bubbles and bits of debris left in the clay pot to explode, and it will be ruined.

When the pot comes out of the furnace and is cooled off, it's painted with glaze, and put back into the furnace again. The glazing process can actually require several excursions back into the furnace before it's completed and the lump of clay finally becomes the thing of beauty the potter envisioned; a pleasure to the eye of all who see it.

Just as with my paintings, the making is a process. Creating anything out of clay requires both a strong mental vision and patience for a potter. There's a lot of mess, and there's stress, pressure, and urgency all before the purpose makes sense to the onlooker. The whole process of forming an *objet d'art* is relatively unpleasant from the viewpoint of the materials being used in its creation—you could even say downright painful. The beauty part only comes when the process is completed.

The Master Creator

The Master Creator talks about himself as a potter. We are God's creations, and he is our maker. He's the one who has the vision and patience to get us through the process of our life-forming to the point where it will make sense to us.

The Lord has made all things for himself. (4)

I personally struggled with this concept for years, especially when I read about the potter and the clay in the Bible: "Shall the thing formed say to him that formed it, Why have you made me thus?" (5) And I realized that's exactly what my heart was saying. I had a number of disagreements with God about the way I was being made. My thoughts were often on this line: 'There are many praiseworthy people in the world, and I'm not like any of them. What's that all about?' Then I read: "Doesn't the potter have power over the clay, of the same lump to make one vessel unto honor, and another unto dishonor?" (6) I concluded that I must be one of the lumps destined for dishonor, and on a very deep level, I lived with sadness and a sense of not being good enough for decades.

As I have come to know God better, I realize he does *everything* well. That includes making me. The Bible says "You have created all things, and for Your pleasure they are and were created." (7) He made us the way we are for his own pleasure. He enjoys us. Go figure, right?

It seems obvious to me that God doesn't create junk—an extremely intelligent, systematic God who only makes things that please him wouldn't make something worthless. As an artist, I never would.

God puts purpose into everything he creates. So when I was thinking I was a nothing, I was actually contradicting God. The Bible says everything God does is marvelously done. (8) Therefore it follows that He made me marvelously too, and I've decided if what I am pleases him, I'm going to go with it and be myself.

I find myself more and more becoming engaged in discovering and following the passions of my own heart without comparing myself unfavorably to people I see around me. I still can't see how everything about myself is marvelously done. It still looks messy and disjointed at times. But for now, I am willing to concede the point to God, and wait to see how it all pans out. I am okay viewing myself as a work in progress.

More of the Creator's marvelous work

In looking at the wonders of the universe and the intricacies of nature, one can't help but see that there is system and purpose in all of creation. There really are no random bits of chaos, you merely have to be looking on the right scale to see the patterns.

The evidence of God's wonderful working is all around us, if we will take the time to see it. Wonders come in all sizes and shapes and they are everywhere. If we look closely, we can see tiny wonders on a microscopic scale—like the unending beauty and variety of snowflake patterns.

Think for a moment about plain, everyday water. Water is vital as rain, nourishing the earth and causing its seeds to grow, yet with a simple change in temperature, plain raindrops can become infinitely-varied snowflakes drifting gently down, or the ice balls of hail pummeling the earth.

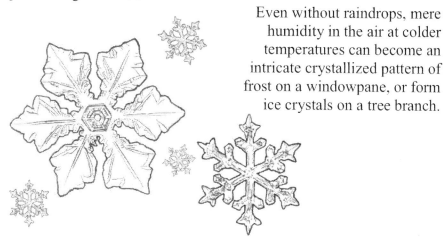

Even without raindrops, mere humidity in the air at colder temperatures can become an intricate crystallized pattern of frost on a windowpane, or form ice crystals on a tree branch.

One of the most incredible sights I've ever seen in my life was the pattern made by a rare winter storm freezing rain onto a long-needled pine tree around the corner from my house. It kept raining and quick-freezing, raining and quick-freezing, building ice up on the branches, turning them into living lace. Stunning! When I saw it, I just stood and stared in spite of the extreme cold. I would just about have given body parts for the use of a camera in that moment.

Ask yourself, if plain water becomes this intricately wonderful by just changing temperature, what other wonders are all around us that we haven't noticed? Watch the sunrise or a sunset; watch the patterns the clouds make. Watch the lightning flash across the sky during a rainstorm. If you don't have great weather happening in your area of the world, the Internet is full of amazing weather photographs. Take some time to look, and be amazed at the awesome visual displays of extreme weather.

Or walk outside at night and look at the stars. There are wonders on an unbelievably grand scale in the heavens. Look at some of the photos that were taken by the Hubble telescope. (http://hubblesite.org/) Find a picture of our own galaxy, in which our sun and whole solar system are not even big enough to show up as a pin-sized dot on the picture. Then consider that scientists are now saying there are over 200 billion *galaxies* in the universe—how vast a number of stars are there in 200 billion galaxies? It boggles the mind.

*The universe begins to look more like a
great thought than like a great machine.*
James Jeans (Astronomer)

As immense as the universe has become to us, a Creator by definition must be even bigger. And the more science discovers, the more intelligent the Creator gets, in much the same way a young adult's parents somehow get smarter than they were during that person's teenage years.

"Lift up your eyes on high, and behold who has created these things, that brings out their host by number: he calls them all by names by the greatness of his might, for that he is strong in power; not one fails." (9)

Listen to the same passage from The Message: "Who even comes close to being like God? To whom or what can you compare him? Look at the night skies. Who do you think made all this? Who marches this army of stars out each night, counts them off, calls each by name—so magnificent, so powerful!—and never overlooks a single one? Why would you ever complain or whine, saying, God has lost track of me. He doesn't care what happens to me. Don't you know anything? Haven't you been listening? God doesn't come and go. God *lasts*. He's the Creator of all you can see or imagine. He doesn't get tired out, doesn't pause to catch his breath. And he knows *everything*, inside and out."

The Creator is so invested in what he has made, that he holds everything in place while all the parts accomplish their individual purposes. That's an outlay of power on a magnitude and scope beyond imagining! And this is the Creator who made *you*.

You are extremely valuable.

What determines the value of valuable things? The dictionary says value is the relative worth determined by a medium of exchange—in other words, value is determined by the amount of money or other

valuable commodity someone is willing to pay for it. The value of items in a store is set by their price. If you purchase a famous, one-of-a-kind painting, the last price which was paid provides the base for determining its current value, right? Its present value is a combination of what was paid last time, and how much more someone is willing to pay for it now.

For you are bought with a price
(10)

Even though you're still a work in progress, you're more valuable than you know. The price that was paid for you is what determines your value, not the voice of "not good enough" with which self-worth speaks out of your subconscious mind's depths.

The magnificent Creator who has the sheer imagination and intelligence to create 200 billion galaxies, and the strength and ability to keep every part of all of it in order and functioning, paid the ultimate price for you. That makes you *extremely* valuable.

Here's another passage from the Bible to show you how involved God *already is* in your life:

"O Lord, you have examined my heart and know everything about me. You know when I sit down or stand up. You know my thoughts even when I'm far away.

"You see me when I travel and when I rest at home. You know everything I do. You know what I am going to say even before I say it, Lord. You go before me and follow me. You place your hand of blessing on my head. Such knowledge is too wonderful for me, too great for me to understand!

"I can never escape from your Spirit! I can never get away from your presence! If I go up to heaven, you are there; if I go down to the grave, you are there. If I ride the wings of the morning, if I dwell by the farthest oceans, even there your hand will guide me, and your strength will support me. I could ask the darkness to hide me and the light around me to become night—but even in darkness I cannot hide from you. To you the night shines as bright as day. Darkness and light are the same to you.

"You made all the delicate, inner parts of my body and knit me together in my mother's womb. Thank you for making me so wonderfully complex! Your workmanship is marvelous—how well I know it. You watched me as I was being formed in utter seclusion, as I was woven together in the dark of the womb. You saw me before I was born.

"Every day of my life was recorded in your book. Every moment was laid out before a single day had passed. How precious are your thoughts about me, O God. They cannot be numbered! I can't even count them; they outnumber the grains of sand! And when I wake up, you are still with me!

Search me, O God, and know my heart; test me and know my anxious thoughts. Point out anything in me that offends you, and lead me along the path of everlasting life." (11)

There are only two ways to live your life: one as though nothing is a miracle, the other as though everything is.

Albert Einstein

We think of Albert Einstein as a stereotypical scientist-type who had little time for God, but "his professional journey brought him to a personal epiphany in which he proclaimed that the more he understood the universe, the more he believed that a Creator was at work." (12) Can you entrust yourself yet to the care of the immensely capable Creator? He has invested a lot into you already, and put a huge value on you. Don't you think that he's willing to help you realize your potential? Ask God to help you with your dreams.

৪৩ Chapter 13: A Fresh Perspective of My Life Experiences

To gain new insight and perspective on our life experiences, we will need to look at how we can re-transcribe painful memories and in the process literally rewire our brains, so we will never see those memories in the same way, or feel the same pain we've felt every time we remember them ever again.

Our subconscious mind holds all our memories; everything that has ever happened to us recorded in vivid, big-as-life detail. It's all still there, every detail, just like when we lived it. Think of the instances you've seen on TV, heard or read about where amazing details not consciously remembered came out of someone's subconscious mind under hypnotic suggestion.

If we consider the whole of our memory as "territory"—a geographical map of our life experiences—then we can see there are individual points on the map where significant events occurred. I said earlier that I call those memories "signpost moments."

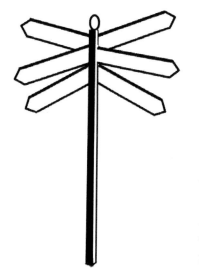

Every strongly emotional event that occurs in our life creates a signpost moment in our memory. This is true for both our good times and our traumatic times. These signposts are hammered into the ground of our memory landscape and given their initial significance by the strong emotion which was involved in those events.

As time moves on for us, each time our memory revisits that event, we feel a new present-tense emotion for a historical event that only exists in our memories. Our present emotion is received by our subconscious mind as new input, attached to the memory for the next time it comes round to our attention, and pulling that historical memory into our "now."

Each new emotional impulse is like attaching another arm onto our signpost. Picture each memory adding another arm to the signpost of Pain, Shame, Guilt. The more times we remember, and feel a fresh emotional twinge, the bigger our signpost becomes.

It's not the happy memories that we revisit in our minds either, is it? It seems to be the memory of pain that rehearses itself most often in our memories. Imagine the focus that is building in you with incident after incident of additional pain added on top of the original trauma. The problem is that this emotional buildup *draws* our attention to these memories, the same way a person can't seem to help touching where they've have put a Band-Aid. Or like moths to a light—it's a painful and sometimes lethal attraction.

After awhile these signpost moments are such a huge focus, and the emotion that holds them in place is so deeply imbedded that they become part of our reality. They come back and rehearse themselves in our minds involuntarily, continually imprinting themselves into the subconscious mind as a bigger and stronger focus, so that with time, they are a key part of what identifies us. Have you ever met a person for the first time, and you could just *see* something of what they'd lived through on them, even if there was no obvious physical clue or scar? Their signpost moments are showing.

Our focuses affect our future

Our signpost focuses act as directives for the subconscious mind. And the bigger the signpost—that is, the more often we remember it with feeling—the stronger the focus. Who would consciously choose to have a focus directing their future to include their past pain, shame and guilt?

That's the danger of leaving negative signpost memories alone to continue to grow bigger and therefore stronger. They have the ability to affect our present life and our identity as well as our entire future.

Signpost moments work like self-fulfilling prophecies. Every time we add another instance of remembering, with the strong feelings the memory triggers in us, thereby increasing the emotional emphasis of that signpost moment, we are directing our subconscious mind to *make it happen again* more urgently.

When a current circumstance triggers that signpost moment, our thinking goes something like this: "I've seen something similar before." It may not even be a conscious awareness or thought. Along with that conscious or subconscious awareness (it could be either or both) is a surge of emotion, "Yuck!" or "Eughh!" or "Oww!" And our present reaction is going to be stronger than might be warranted by the circumstances triggering it. We will probably find ourselves over-reacting, without really knowing why we're doing it.

Our decisions from that point on will be to protect ourselves from the associated pain, which may have no real counterpart in the actual situation; it may be all in our subconscious mind. But our decisions now will be faulty, and what they are trying to protect us from, the huge "focus" in our subconscious mind will actually *draw to us* and cause it to happen over and over again.

> *Everything in my life is reclaimable as a good thing that will contribute to my dream.*
>
> Tracey Armstrong

Reclaim your signpost moments

There is a way to reclaim your traumatic signpost moments as good, healthy places in your memory which will not reach forward to sabotage your future success in life. There is a way to draw out the built-up poison of so much painful emotion.

The Bible says God has only good intentions for us: "For I know the plans I have for you, declares the Lord, plans for wholeness and not for evil, to give you a future and a hope." (1) But it also addresses that bad things do happen, and for those who allow him, God turns those bad things around and changes the end result of them: "And we know that God causes everything to work together for the good

127

of those who love God and are called according to his purpose for them." (2) So the things God intends for our future are good and He also transforms everything that happens to us into good.

Hindsight tends to prove this out. Hindsight always gives a much different view of our lives than we have in the middle of the fray. The Bible says "Surely goodness and mercy shall follow me all the days of my life." (3) Looking back in retrospect at our lives, goodness and mercy are what we see.

If the historical view of our lives only shows the goodness and mercy, what would it be like to live in that awareness in the present? How differently would we be able to live if we truly *expected only good things to happen* for us in our future lives?

It's very hard to see a pattern of any sort without the proper perspective. The repeating emotions we put to our recalled memories tend to make them seem more immediate, closer than they really are in linear time. So when we're trying to see our life patterns, sometimes we need to put a little emotional distance between ourselves and a traumatic event in our life, in order to be able to see it in perspective.

Find the rainbow part

It has been said that in every awful thing that happens to us, with a different perspective, we can find an *equivalent good* in that thing. (4) There is some hidden good that came out of that catastrophe in your life. *Find it* Find the good in your memories. This is the first step in rewriting your history. We're going to look at how we can reprogram our memories, and unstick our stuck emotional places, dismantling hidden traps that would otherwise impact our futures.

I once found a photograph online of the mother of all storms: black, wicked-looking clouds swirling around, and lightning flashing. Yet there was a small rainbow on the edge of the clouds. Rainbows traditionally speak of hope and promise; they are never about destruction or calamity.

So when you look back at the traumas in your life, look for the rainbow part.

> *Try this:* 1. Make a list of the strongly emotional events of your life, good and bad, as far back as you can remember.
> Give each one a score, "1" meaning I didn't feel much of anything, to 10 being the strongest emotion. Use +1 through +10 for the positive events, and -1 through -10 for negative events.
> 2. Then take a piece of blank paper on which you've drawn a horizontal line through the middle, and map your life events, as the example shows below in Chart 10A.
> 3. Put in the **feelings you have now** when you think about each of your -10 and +10 life events, writing them under your brief description of each event. These are your emotional markers, your soul's signpost memories. These highs and lows set the parameters of your expectations for your future life.

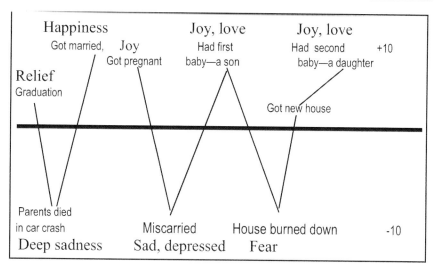

Chart 10A: Life Map with present emotions

I do want to say here, it's important that when you look at what your heart will show you, step outside the emotions you've attached to the events and use your self-awareness to look calmly, like it wasn't you but was happening to someone else. Picture yourself watching the memories of your life on a television screen, like a TV movie of your life played by actors. This is possible—think of the example of Viktor Frankl quoted earlier in Chapter 5. I doubt that you are living through an emotional and physical hell to the same degree he did, yet he not only survived the Nazi death camp, but while he was undergoing torture he gained new skill in imagining, without his emotions and extreme pain shutting down his ability to step outside his circumstances and see a future good place in his mind. His visualizing gave him the strength to endure, so that he lived to fulfill what he had seen, and share his experiences with his college classes.

In every "bad" event of your life, there *is* something of value which is important for you to find, which will be useful to your future, and may even be an integral part of your dream. For example, if you've come out of abuse, if you've survived extreme hardship of any kind, guess what you're passionate about stopping in other people's lives? Your passions are what fuel your dream.

One woman I know, Joan, lived with decades of verbal abuse, which had the effect in her life of isolating her, restricting her into an increasingly smaller and smaller box. She had to continually choose to suppress her own thoughts, ideas, wishes and words for a non-confrontational place of peace and safety. Where she was a strongly self-confident young woman, over time Joan lost her dreams and her self-confidence, and she wasn't even aware how great a loss she was experiencing. Yet today she is dreaming again; and she is a successful life-coach who is passionately helping people to reclaim their confidence in themselves and to live their fullest imaginable lives, no matter what their life experience may have been.

Rename your memories

Lasting changes will never come from merely changing your circumstances. Think of all the lottery winners who after a short time find themselves as poor as ever. Lasting changes require pulling your subconscious resources into the positive future you choose for yourself, and changing how you think on your deepest subconscious level. Changed thinking *always* results in life changes, and the more solidly imprinted the different thinking is within your subconscious mind, that is the measure to which you can expect to *keep* your newly changed actions and habits.

This sounds like a complicated process, but it's actually fairly simple. The first key is to rename all your signpost moments. Find one good thing out of each experience, and call that something in your past by a *different name*.

Call a whole season of your life "The time I learned (*something good*)," or "The time (*something good, or some good purpose or good life focus*) first occurred to me", or if nothing else "The time I learned how strong my will to survive is." Make your new names as strongly positive and good as you are able.

Renaming our dreaded signpost memories changes the way our subconscious mind handles them. We're able to finally release the excessive emotions attached to our signposts and forgive whoever and whatever is exposed. This defuses our signpost focuses, and prevents them from becoming even bigger problems in the future. "The emotions that you're able to experience can bring a recollection to the surface; if your feelings are suppressed, however, they can bury that same memory far below your awareness, where it can affect your perceptions, decisions, behavior, and even health, all unconsciously." (5)

Once released, however, our creative imagination gets a huge boost as our signposts begin to sink back into the benign fabric of our memory landscape. Our reproductive imagination takes its proper place as the repository of our history instead of the front-line leadership role it has had in our lives, by which it was effectively pulling our dread expectations out of the past and dragging them into our future.

Leaving signpost memories in place is the equivalent of carrying live land-mines around in your body—it could have huge health implications at some point in the future. Anyone recognize — "This always seems to happen to me," or "that runs in our family, so I don't know why I should expect any different?" These statements are indicators of the presence of a negative expectation on a deep subconscious level, a signpost in our lives with huge reproductive capacity, dominating and leading our expectations and locking us in to negative future events.

> *Try this:* This next part will take some careful thought, but if you will do it, the results can be dramatically life-changing. Find that good that came out of your deeply negative events, and *cross out* the name you gave the event on your timeline, then *write in* a new name chosen for the good you discovered out of that event.
> Example: Chart 10B: Life Map New Names

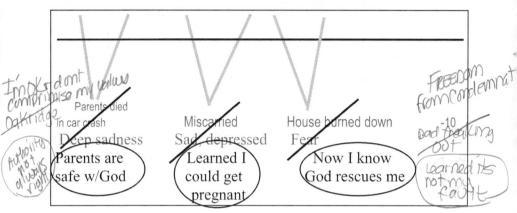

Chart 12 B: Life Map New Names

By renaming them, the emotional markers that used to determine our reactions to new events and keep our expectations *chained* to probable near repetitions of those past unsuccessful events—these signposts will begin to recede back from the strong focus they've been, thereby losing their power to influence our future. If we will diligently call past experiences by the new name we have given them, it will reduce our fear level and apprehension for the future, and enable us to see more good possibilities instead of fearful outcomes ahead for us.

Our creative imagination can provide more positive possibilities with the reproductive imagination following meekly behind it, rather than trying to dominate our mental image of our future by incessantly rehearsing past events.

So—take the time to look as deeply as you can at the signposts in your subconscious mind. When you identify another area of wrong focus, name it something different, for the good you pull out of that moment of your history. You'll soon *feel* the release.

Rewrite my history

We can rewrite our history—that is to say, we cannot literally change the events that have already happened, but we can totally change how they affect us, how they live on in our subconscious mind's memory and thereby influence our present and our future. When we are just starting in this process of rewriting our memories, they will still speak the same old refrains to us. We need to handle our remembering differently—by pointing out to ourselves that this event brought something good to us and is now called "(*your new name for it*)" every time it comes to mind.

By renaming our signpost memories, we are changing our probable future. Deliberately rehearse those new names for things out loud and often. Whenever something reminds you of that memory event, call it *again* what you have renamed it. Say its new name out loud. When we hear it, we believe it; that's just how human beings are made. From now on, *never refer to that event by any other name.*

If you will do this, deliberately turning your thoughts forward, and refusing to look backward and dwell on what is in the past, you should begin to experience a lightness, a release, and a new hope emerging. Dread and anxiety should start melting away. You should find it easier to put your creative imagination to work and start imagining your best life. You should find yourself increasingly able to focus ahead on your future with a happy anticipation. Whenever you have a free moment, continue to ask yourself "What do I really want?"

I have walked out this renaming memories road and I know from personal experience how effective it is. There was something in my own past so painful I couldn't make myself face it to search for anything good that came from it. Then someone suggested imagining something else happening than what did happen, inserting a new *possibility* into my *history*. I tried it. When I applied a possibility to the closed-in memory that was holding me down, it felt like a key going into a lock. I felt something being released and it was such a vivid sensation I could almost hear it click. And the teeth went out of that memory. It stopped gnawing on me, and I was eventually able to face it and rename it and leave it behind me.

I have taken a number of people through the same process, and every time it has brought real freedom. I know it can work for you too, from wherever you are.

Take courage. Rename some life moments, and let the light of new hope begin shining through your whole life. Rewrite the history of your life, so that it all contributes to your future dreams.

Declaration #14: I choose what identifies me. It is what I say it is.

෩ Chapter 14: A Fresh Perspective of My Purpose

Focus forward

Forward is the direction in which we were created to think, the direction in which we can see possibilities and new ideas instead of memory reruns. We are wired to be positive, and we work best in positive possibilities. It's a lovely atmosphere to live in.

However, be forewarned: our best life will not present itself to us all at once. It's been shut down and diverted into the limitations of compromise too long. We have to coax out the details of a satisfying future by thinking about our best life a lot. The more details we can imagine, the more excited we will become by our imagined new possibilities. This is the positive way to make a strong focus of what has not yet existed but is surely now begun to come our way. With our imagined thoughts, we are actually changing our brain structure; we are *building expectations* that will make our brains able to stay more focused on possibilities. Even more than our imagination, I say that these visualized expectations are everything. This is our focused hope actively causing our brains to be enlarged to accommodate our new dreams.

> *Even more than imagination, I say expectation is everything.*
> *Expectation is your focused hope.*

Resolutely keep looking forward and mentally reaching for more details of what you are imagining. Keep a *My Best Life* journal within reach, and record the new things you add to your future possibilities as you see them. Write it, draw it, or cut out pictures from magazines that are close to what you want. Put what you have written, drawn or cut out somewhere you can look at it every day.

Our comfort zones have a conflicting voice to this new imagination place. The flawed reality bits that provide the walls and ceilings of our comfort zone try to limit our imagination projections into our future life. So whenever you have need to shake free of the limitations of your comfort zone, remind your reproductive memory what its signposts have been renamed. Say their new names out loud, emphatically. Then put them firmly behind you again. Relegate the past to the past, including the limitations of your comfort zone, and start talking to yourself in possibility language. Tell your heart that the door is open to a new future and this is a good thing.

Focus exclusively on seeing and imagining what's ahead, which will be so overwhelmingly satisfying that the unsettling feeling of having your comfort zone shaken up a bit will prove to be worth the temporary internal discomfort.

> *Problems are only opportunities in work clothes.*
> Henry J. Kaiser

In fact, it's good to put everything that has happened behind you, both good and bad, and *live forward* all the time. The Apostle Paul said it this way in the Bible: "but one thing I do: forgetting what is behind me and straining forward toward what lies ahead, I keep pursuing the goal..." (1)

When things happen

When new traumatic events happen to you, don't wait until they become big, messy, ugly signposts before you slap a positive new name on them. Start looking for something good to come out of it right away. As soon as you can recognize it, name the experience according to that good thing. By working this process, you are closing the door on that memory's ability to hold you captive in a painful place. It becomes a closed deal that has no more ruling power over you, leaving you free to move ahead in life. We should never let fears hold us back from pursuing our hopes, or let our past overshadow our bright tomorrow.

Step away from fears

Don't let fear of the unknown stop you from moving into your best life. It will try. Here's a good visual exercise to use: when a person is still sitting or leaning on a fence, whatever is on either side can easily reach them or get their attention at any time. On the one side is the future, with all of its unlimited possibilities. On the other side is the voice of our experience that fears the unknown, and prefers the limitations of memory as being familiar to the point of feeling comfortable. We are standing on the future side of the fence, but which direction are we facing?

If we truly want the better new, and we don't want what is on the other side of the fence, i.e. to be held back by the old fearful voices that hold to the safety of familiar territory, even if it was not good, then the answer is simple. We should step away from the fence. Turn our back to the past and move forward, focusing on the future. The voices of the past will recede and grow fainter the more forward progress we make.

Finding my life purpose

We've gotten a better feeling for who we are, what our identity is, and the next step is to find our purpose for being who we are.

> *When you have a sense of your own identity and a vision*
> *of where you want to go in your life, you then have*
> *the basis for reaching out to the world and*
> *going after your dreams for a better life.*
>
> Stedman Graham

Maybe you already know what you're passionate about, and where you want to spend your life's efforts. Or maybe you're unsure about these things. Most of us haven't spent enough time considering "What do I really want?"

Try this: Make three lists for yourself, using the qualifying factors of *"if neither money or time were an issue"*: What do I want to be? What do I want to do? What do I want to have? Write it all down.

There are a number of formulas for finding your purpose available online, some free. Use one of these to create a purpose statement for yourself, otherwise known as a "mission statement."

1. Nightingale Conant, a world leader in personal development since

1960, has a free Mission Statement builder:
http://www.nightingale.com/mission_select.aspx

2. FranklinCovey also has an online template you can fill in to generate a mission statement, and they will email it to you when you're done: **http://www.franklincovey.com/msb/** They give you a choice of building a personal, a family or a team statement.

If you find yourself stuck for the right words, check out this web source: **http://cmorse.org/missiongen/**
This is a Mission Statement Generator with groups of adverbs, verbs, adjectives and nouns that may fit into a purpose statement.

If you want to hear someone else explain just what a mission statement is and how to make one, try this site:
http://www.ask.com/questions-about/Personal-Mission-Statement-Generator

> *Always dream and shoot higher than you know how to.*
> *Don't bother just to be better than your contemporaries*
> *or predecessors. Try to be better than yourself.*
>
> William Faulkner

Or go to The Permission to Dream Book's website: **permissiontodreambook.com**. Download **My Life Purpose**, and do that one. This will give you a starting point, a direction to start considering for your future. You will want to begin using your purpose statement like a new pair of reality glasses, and look at every part of your life through the corrected lens of your purpose. Finding your purpose is a REAL paradigm shift!!

You are made with the capacity for greatness in you. Who knows that famous quote, "If you believe it, you can become it?" (2) The Bible says: "Jesus said unto him, If you can believe, all things are possible to him that believes." (3) Believe it.

Keep pushing the limits of your dream. Dreams and purpose are so much bigger than who you are now. They're supposed to be. Start by dreaming, and let God show you that impossible dreams are what you're intended to dream. If you don't start by dreaming it, you won't have a prayer of ever becoming it.

> *The only way to discover the limits of the possible*
> *is to go beyond them into the impossible.*
>
> Arthur C. Clarke

Sow into your purpose

Put in the mental work of projecting yourself into that future new life structure described in the beginning of this chapter. It's sowing, and in the same way that seeds surely grow, there will be a crop of results—bits of your purpose will start showing up all over the landscape of your life. "So many of our dreams at first seem impossible, then they seem improbable, and then, when we summon the will, they soon become inevitable." (4) If you don't relate to the idea of sowing seeds, think of it in another way: it's cause and effect. Like snow building up to an inevitable avalanche, thinking possibilities and repeatedly visualizing your dreams also will bring predictable results. For what seems a long time there is no visible change, then suddenly *everything* changes.

Keep sowing seeds of hope-full possibility thinking into your future dream. Daily. And start anticipating the "suddenly" that's surely ahead.

Do things differently NOW

Start to pay attention to your present circumstances in a different way. See "now" in the light of what you are envisioning for your future. There are things you can do and say right now while maintaining the forward focus that will contribute to your dream and to the things into which you are starting to imagine yourself. DO those, *whether you feel like it or not.*

Look for parts of your possibilities to begin to show up in your "now." Gather those to you and whatever the requirement of these new things, do it, whether you feel like the whole of your possibilities will really happen or not. Keep sowing into your hope.

> *POSSIBILITIES: The greatest waste in the world is the difference between what we are and what we could become.*
>
> Ben Herbster

Here's a synopsis for repossessing your future best life:

1. FOCUS ahead. Imagine your best life. Get really detailed about it.

2. Write it, draw it, or cut out pictures from magazines that are similar to what you want.

3. Make declarations you can speak out loud.

4. Put your declarations where you can see them every day. Speak them out loud every day with feeling!!

5. Put everything from the past behind you, good and bad.

6. When you have the need, remind your reproductive memory what its memories have been renamed, and then put them behind you again.

7. Resolutely keep looking forward. Force your attention forward whenever it gets distracted.

8. Do something every day towards your best life.

Look at your purpose with the same kind of unwavering focus as an eagle or hawk who has his eye on prey and is moving out of the sky with all speed to obtain it. Keep your eye on your purpose, with every part of you centered on reaching that goal. Don't stop looking until you get there.

What are some things you can do today, this week, toward your dream? Put the list on this page into action, even if it's just a tiny action. It will give you a surprisingly strong boost of confidence.

This works!

I've been teaching this material with significant success at the Union Gospel Mission (UGM) in Seattle, Washington for 6 plus years at the time of this writing. When I got to this point in the class, one of my students last year (2011) really took it to heart and put action to it. She made a collage picturing the things she wanted, brought it to class to show me, and then put it on her wall at home where she would see it daily.

Here's her story: I have four kids, who were one, three, four and five years old when I came to UGM. I was divorced, coming out of domestic violence. "I was dead on the inside. I had my faith in God, but I had no hope." She graduated my class, and the year-long program at UGM, and is now interning there. She says her kids are calmer, that her time at UGM has made room for them to be children. She said her goal picture is working for her: "I do something every day towards it. I'm about to make a new one." She's gotten housing, a pictured family vacation is about to happen, she's taken the kids on mini-trips for fun, she has a job she loves, her bills are paid, and she's tithing again. College is still in the future, but I have no doubt she will get there. I couldn't be prouder. I know the things I've been teaching work, because I myself walk in them, but it pops my buttons to hear my students reporting good things.

Another woman who was in my third class of The Permission to Dream Book six years ago is now working on staff at UGM as a case manager. She said "Just the title spoke to me. I needed that permission. I needed to know it was okay to dream again."

Declaration #15: My life has purpose. I am not here by accident.

This is the true joy in life, the being used for a purpose recognized by yourself as a mighty one; the being thoroughly worn out before you are thrown on the scrap heap; the being a force of nature instead of a feverish selfish little clod of ailments and grievances complaining that the world will not devote itself to making you happy.

Section Four:
Moving Forward

In this last section, we will pull all the things we've learned together and take another run at life, with a new hope of actually realizing our best life.

ങ൫ Chapter 15: Building Right This Time

You spend all your life engineering a dream. When it gets lost, you have to start over again restructuring, re-engineering.

Tracey Armstrong

Anytime a person sets out to build something new, if that person is wise, they will start with a solid foundation. In a literal sense, this involves surveying the ground on which the building is to sit, identifying the issues and conditions on both the surface and below-ground, and dealing with them. If there are inherent weaknesses in the ground, like a subterranean spring that could undermine the structure once it was built, or bad drainage patterns that could lead to surrounding area runoff draining down into the new building, these things must be dealt with before building begins.

The same principle holds true for your restructured life. If you've repeatedly experienced failure or obstacles showing up in similar ways over the years, try to identify what is the commonality to these occasions. Is there a fear of failure? A fear of success? A feeling of "not worthy of succeeding?" A comfort zone that is about to be broken? Is there a life label that speaks out of your subconscious when you are nearing a breakthrough success, for instance "It's going too good. Nothing goes this good for me."

Still talking about preparing literal ground: if there is a flaw in the ground, a corrective measure must be set in place to offset it. If there is a bad reputation, a label of "unbuildable," it must be explored and debunked, so that the builder and everyone in the future who has occasion to use the building may have confidence in its stability.

Once the ground is prepped, work begins on the foundation. The taller the structure will eventually be, the deeper and stronger the foundation must be. An elementary rule of building is complete the foundation first, then build the superstructure.

I did a search of skyscraper foundations being dug to see what is involved with setting a proper foundation under a spectacularly tall structure. I found photos and a commentary on one skyscraper in the beginning stages of construction which said the foundation would be nearly 100 feet deep when it was done, before an inch of building would be visible above ground. For us, there's a huge perspective-setting lesson in this. The bigger your dream, the more preparation must go into its foundation.

> *If you have built castles in the air, your work need not be lost; that is where they should be. Now put the foundations under them.*
> Henry David Thoreau

There are no short-cuts. You decide how your future life will look, how high you are aiming, what it will take to maximize your potential.

Then realize that before you build up where it's visible to others from a distance, you have to finish laying a proper foundation under your dream. Give yourself the time it takes to build a proper foundation for your future. The internal discovery process you've begun while reading this book will continue; it will take time to thoroughly heal. This deep inner work of healing and resetting your expectations *is* the foundation of your dream. The more thoroughly you invest into correcting the issues and laying a proper (*healed*) foundation, the more spectacular your life can become and remain. I want you to move into your future and build stable successes on a solid foundation of hope and confidence.

> *Only he who can see the invisible can do the impossible.*
> Frank Gaines

In the rest of this chapter we're going to talk about the blueprints for your future. Setting goals and actions steps will be the lines and dimensions that make up your life blueprint. Even while you are in the digging process and working on the foundation under your life plans, don't lose your focus. Keep your eyes on the goals, not on the underground issues. The contractors who build skyscrapers have the blueprints in front of them constantly, even while they're digging the holes and pouring the concrete of foundations far below ground level. It's the reason they are able to stay focused without being discouraged by all the foundation work and issues.

Growing hope

Hope is the precursor to faith, and faith is an action-motivator. Faith gathers evidence for what we're hope-expecting, and when enough evidence is in hand, steps out into action.

We've explored what hope is, that it is necessary to life, and that we put our hope in whatever we expect will satisfy us. We saw that we can put our hope in things and in people, and I suggested that like the Bible says, it's perhaps best to "put your hope in God." (1)

I want to talk about one aspect of the definition of faith for a moment. Faith is universal to all mankind, whether a person is religious or not. We *all* have faith. Faith is simply what we believe in and act on. We don't all put our faith in God. We put our faith in many things. We put our faith in our fears sometimes. We put our faith in chaos or confusion. We put our faith in poverty. We put our faith in family dysfunction. We put our faith in our relationships turning out badly. We put our faith in *whatever we expect*. Expecting is the action of faith and we all do it.

> *Yes, you can be a dreamer and a doer too, if you will remove one word from your vocabulary. Impossible.*
> Robert Schuller

Hope sees into the invisible realm of possibility. When enough evidence of what we're hoping for has been collected, faith makes our hope manifest itself and be tangible in the visible realm we live in. You cannot have the motivating confidence of faith without a strong hope. When our possibility-seeing hope has been made visible by a strong confidence, there's a point where we easily move into some kind of action. That's the place where hope has tipped over into a place of assurance from which faith can step out. Faith is a sureness that compels us into action, confidant that the action will be successful. Faith is what propels Olympic athletes into the going-beyond actions that win gold medals.

This brings me to something I call *now faith*. We've seen that hoping against hope can take us through life's deserts. If hope is the water of life that keeps you going through dry places, then *"now faith"* is the ICE ROAD, able to hold up the 20 ton weight of your big dreams moving forward over impossible road places. (Who in their right mind builds a road for mega-ton freight trucks to travel on nothing but the *ocean*, for goodness' sake?)

You can make anything happen if you commit to it and take action.
Anthony Robbins

Let's summarize the process of building hope into this Now-I-CAN-do-it confidence, step by step:

1. Keep building your hope level with deliberate possibility thinking and speaking. Rehearse your dream out loud frequently.

2. Pay attention to what you are hearing—we get faith (confidence) by hearing. [2] Only let yourself hear positive things. Listen to success stories, everywhere you can. This will give you confidence that you can succeed too.

3. Read the Bible. You develop hearing by ingesting the Word. [3]

4. Ask the God of hope to give you confidence in believing. He *wants* you to be so full of hope that it propels you to excel farther than you ever thought was possible. [4]

5. Repeat steps 1-4 until *"now faith"* surges up from within you into confident action.

Declaration #16: I am deliberately and calmly rebuilding what I need to rebuild.

∽∂∝ Chapter 16: Baby Steps Forward

Take your heart's temperature

Your actions are a reflection of your own heart's confidence level. If you want to know where you are now in your process, look at what you are doing, and analyze it. What level of confidence did *that* action exhibit? Don't think you can skip the steps of dealing with your heart's issues and building your hope and still be able to move forward into your best life. If one achieves a measure of success without this foundation work, it would be like winning the lottery without first acquiring the mental, emotional and judgmental skills of wealth-building, i.e. therefore still having the habits and expectations of a poverty mindset—it would almost certainly not be a sustainable success. Permanent and sustainable life changes start with changing the heart's emotional habits, its thinking and beliefs, and most of all its expectations and focus, then reaching out from that changed place to impact circumstances.

All actions are responses to stimuli. What we may see as an original action is actually parts of our physical anatomy responding to an order from somewhere else, the brain or the heart. In chapter 1 we discussed how it used to be thought that the brain was the sole motivator of our actions, but that recent scientific study has shown the heart at the center of the subconscious mind to be the big boss and the brain mind being second in command, rather than the other way around. Most of the time they work together, but when there is a disagreement, the heart always wins.

So the work we have been doing to see, understand and change what's in the heart is actually changing the scope of what will be possible for us in the future. Where once we thought something was not possible because of limitations so deeply buried in the emotional memories of our heart somewhere in our body/mind that we were not even conscious of their existence, now when we move to take our first baby steps toward our best life, we should have a fresh hope saying "This is possible for me. And I don't care if I don't make it with my first effort; I'm going to keep trying until I get there. I can do this thing." Hope has a stubborn strength. Have you ever tried to get a stubborn person to budge from a conviction, or a decision? If so, then you know how strong stubborn can be. Hope is stubborn about keeping us looking forward and focused on the fulfillment of our hopes. Keep building that hope focus, so that confident action can follow in time.

Take some baby steps

Almost up...   I'm gonna do it...   Ha! I'm up...   One step...   two steps....

I had my niece videotape her son Cyrus's first steps for me, and it was very informative. He started by standing beside a picnic table, and working himself hand over hand from one length of the table to the other. Then he launched himself off and took about three steps without anything to hang onto for support. You could tell his balance was very fragile; you could see him wobbling, unsure how to stay upright. But what you did not see was any lack of confidence or fear.

When he did fall down, he immediately looked up with a big grin, as if to say, "Look what I just did!" The above pictures are from the same day, "First Step Day," and you can see that once the idea caught on, of walking being more fun and faster than crawling, there was no stopping him. It still took him three attempts to get upright, and you can see that his walking form is still pretty shaky, but hey, he's walking. He made it a couple of steps again before he fell down. Then he crawled awhile. It was all fun to him.

Take a lesson from the natural order of things: when you take your first baby steps forward into the realm of possibilities and new places, and don't beat yourself up by the inevitable times when you lose your balance and fall down. Just get up to take the next step and move on without a fuss. Babies do it all the time. How horrible would it be if babies just laid on the floor and cried about falling down, and didn't get up to try again!

I heard a success coach say once that "Big steps are made out of a lot of baby steps." That statement encouraged me immensely, when the steps laid out before me seemed bigger than I could manage. We don't have to take individually huge steps to make huge progress. Step out. Take some action towards making your dream happen. The tiniest steps forward will add up, and it's *forward* movement.

Remember that we only have control of the step we are taking right *now*. We can be planning our next step, and we can be reflecting on the ones we've already taken, but we only are *moving* in the present. Learn to walk in new disciplines, new successes, and new habits in the same way babies learn to walk—by not giving up! Baby steps of action will get you into your impossible dream.

> *Goals are dreams with deadlines.*
>
> Diana Scharf Hunt

Goals

Putting a time to your dream takes it out of vague fantasy and wishful thinking, and makes it a concrete goal. A goal is defined as the result or achievement toward which effort is directed, it's our aim, the end result of our action. If we look at the analogy of a runner in a race, the goal is the finish line. It's where the prizes are handed out. It's where the rewards of our actions are.

Knowing that success is within reach, even by baby steps, let's take some deliberate action by *planning out* some of those steps. Set some goals. I like using S.M.A.R.T. goals. [1] This is a commonly used gauge for effective goal-setting.

The S.M.A.R.T. acronym means:

Specific—What exactly will I accomplish by this goal?

Measurable—How will I know when I have reached it?

Achievable—Is achieving this goal realistic with effort and commitment? Have I got the resources to achieve this goal? If not, how will I get them?

Relevant—Why is this goal significant to my life?

Timely—When will this goal be achieved? (2)

Goals need to have each of these qualities in order to be effective motivators, able to move us forward into our desired future. If our goals do not have all these characteristics, they may not have enough hope in them to build belief in a possibility and enable us to step out in a new choice with confident action.

> *Whatever you can do or dream you can, begin it.*
> *Boldness has genius, power and magic in it. Begin it now.*
> Goethe

Goals can be set for what we want to be, what we want to have, what we want to do. It's where we are aiming to achieve something beyond our status quo. If we do not set goals for ourselves, and work toward them, we are essentially defaulting on our choices. We talked about that—it's like letting other things spend our resources and we end up paying the consequences of choices we didn't make.

Goals must be written down. The reason we write out our goals is that it forces our mind to focus clearly on what we want, and to begin the thinking-it-through process that is part of getting us to our purpose. Writing them down brings goals out of the realms of wishful thinking into a more solid place of confident hope with the ability to move us by predetermined steps into the best life that we are learning to imagine and dream for ourselves.

When we have our goals written down in front of us, then we can begin thinking them out and putting action steps to them. We can do this one of two ways, depending on how our thought processes work.

Action Steps

First approach: Working backwards from where we want to go, from the BIG dream we've dreamed. Look at the end result, and picture yourself already living in your dream and work backwards from there by increments to get to the first step, the thing that you can do immediately which will begin moving you in the sure direction of your goals.

Write down your ultimate goal. Ask yourself: "What do I want to achieve, and by what date?" Be specific. Then ask "What milestone do I need to accomplish just before that, in order to achieve that ultimate goal. What has to be in place and what do I have to do, and by when, so that I'm in a position to reach my final objective?"

Keep working backward: "What do I need to complete before that second-to-last goal?" Work back again. "What do I need to do to make sure the previous goal is reached?"

Continue to work back, in the same way, one step at a time, until you identify the very first milestone you need to accomplish. It doesn't matter how small the step; in fact, it's best if it's something you can start working on *now*. I find this method helps me keep myself from discouragement—although all I see are the tiny steps I am doing, I remember the process I worked through and I know all my littlest steps are taking me to my big focus goal. It keeps things in perspective for me.

Second approach: Get an overall picture of your life, of the areas that need improving. Do the exercise in Chart 13. When you see the "room for improvement" areas, think up one improvement you can make in each area that will start you moving out of where you are and point you in the direction of your big dream. What is the first thing you can think of to do? What is the next logical step after that? Each time you think about it, push a little farther in your imagination, to see a little more clearly and in greater detail what you would like.

You can go to <u>The Permission To Dream Book</u> website and download free charts for both of these directions. Don't be afraid to try them both out, until you identify what works best for you. There is no one way it *has* to be done.

After determining the beginning steps, and setting time limits for your goals, don't beat yourself up if you are trying to move into your dream but you "fail" to meet the timing you set. Just set new times.

One thing I hope we've definitively established: the past is the wrong direction to be focusing on. In the Bible, when a city called Sodom was slated to be destroyed for its overwhelming wickedness, a righteous man named Lot who had lived in the city was moving his family out just in the nick of time, and they were all told not to look back. Lot's wife did, and was turned into a pillar of salt. The admonition still holds true for us: Don't look at the past. You won't turn into salt, but looking at the past can paralyze you into inaction and thereby rob you of your best life.

> *Don't worry about failure.*
> *Worry about the chances you miss when you don't even try.* (3)

Keep sowing into your dream, regardless of whatever stormy circumstances seem to be all around you. You never know when your next breakthrough will come. Circumstances will not keep you from the fulfillment of your dreams, but failing to dream certainly can.

We only walk this way once. Put all you've got into it.

Declaration #17: I am taking baby steps into my dreams.

Goal-setting from our current position

Grade your current degree of satisfaction with each of these areas of your life, from 1-10: One meaning "Worst it could be, nowhere to go but up," and 10 meaning "Perfect, needs no improvement."

Personal_____   Education_____
Spiritual_____   Vocation/job_____
Retirement_____   Social_____
Community service_____   Health/mental_____
Recreation/leisure time____   Health/physical_____
Family_____   Marriage_____

Now place your scores on the chart below, with 10 being the outer ends of each line, and 1 being the center where the lines intersect. This will give you a visual image of your life's balance.

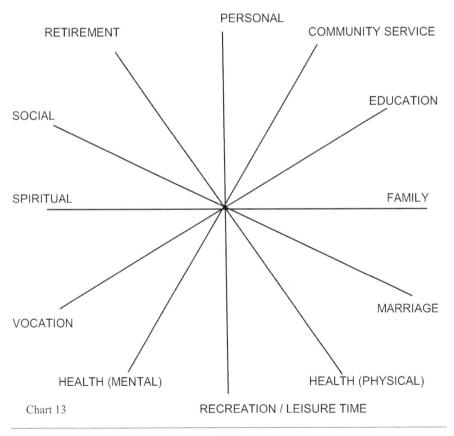

Chart 13

ೞೣೱ Chapter 17: Developing Forward Momentum

Nothing contributes so much to tranquilizing the mind as a steady purpose—a point on which the soul may fix its intellectual eye.

Mary Shelley

A strong and compelling purpose has been a life focus to successful people for centuries, as evidenced by the above quote from Mary Shelley, a talented author who wrote the book <u>Frankenstein</u> at age 17. She lived from 1797 – 1851.

We also have a freshly defined purpose, a new bottom line rule for our lives and we must keep our eyes focused as far ahead as we can see on the road our purpose sets before us. Our purpose is our new prescription for reality glasses. We need to continually re-examine everything in our lives in the light of our purpose. Keep our eyes set on our purpose. Then we won't lose our place, so to speak, in the events that happen day by day. There is a real measure of peace in keeping a steady focus on our purpose.

Purpose is the reason for the *direction* our life takes. To get to our purpose, we break it down into increments, i.e. goals, with corresponding action steps. One step at a time will take us anywhere we choose to go.

The *first step* to doing great things is not to do, but to see.

To build or rebuild our dream we need fresh hope. When we have a growing hope, we begin to spend time imagining future possibilities, rather than past failures or signpost trauma moments. The second part of building our dream is imagining new possibilities. The third component of dreaming is new choices being made out of the pool of our imagined new possibilities. The fourth step is strengthening our new choices by what we say out loud repeatedly with strong feeling, until they are so strong they compel us into confident action.

The *first step* to doing great things is not to do, but to see. When we get a picture of what we want, and hear our hope telling us it's possible for us, we begin to imagine possibilities, and make new choices. And we're well on the way to what we want before we've even lifted a finger in physical activity. Then we put our focus on the action steps we've laid out for ourselves, that as far as we can determine today will take us to our purpose, and begin doing something *now*, realizing it is moving us forward toward the satisfaction of our purpose. Living deliberately this way is keeping our eyes on the blueprints while working in the building of our life structure. And knowing that we are moving toward fulfillment by what we are doing keeps hope nourished and growing in us.

> *Obstacles are those frightful things you see*
> *when you take your eyes off your goal.*
>
> Henry Ford

Obstacles

We have absolute control over our choices, as we've seen, but we don't choose everything that we encounter or all that may show up in our pathways. Even when obstacles present themselves, it's a matter of focus. We simply *do not focus* on those things that get in our way and can so easily distract us.

I'm not saying we don't see what is there, and do whatever we can to deal with it. But we deal with the obstacle without taking our eyes off our goals, or allowing our emotions to be engaged. We don't stop to admire and pay homage to obstacles by being fearful.

We *relentlessly* keep our eyes on our purpose, focusing forward into the realm of hope and possibilities, regardless of the circumstances we find ourselves in. For awhile, this may be a pretty constant tug-of-war—the mental habits we're trying to break (of focusing on past experiences as the gauge for understanding current or potential situations) have a loud voice. The urge to look backward for understanding is strong. That's comfort zone territory, i.e. even if it was awful, it's *familiar*.

We're building new mental and emotional responses to everything in our lives, remember, seeing everything through the filter of our life's purpose. It takes time to build mental habits, the same as any other kind of habit. Twenty-one days of repetition seems to be the minimum to build a new habit, and longer until the new activity happens without conscious effort. Use your absolute right of self-awareness, which enables you to stand apart from the emotion of your life and keep evaluating things and making further choices without drama, simply because they are the best choices for you.

Pay attention to what we're feeding our brains.

You've heard the expression "Garbage in, garbage out?" Instead of allowing our mind to be like a garbage dump for everything that comes our way, we should do what teenagers seem to do naturally—practice selective listening. Listen to what we choose to hear, and ignore the rest.

Pay attention to what you're listening to—and who you're listening to. Stop listening to negative things—and gossip is a negative thing. It hurts us because it builds up deep inside us in invisible but very real places. And stop listening to dreamstealers, past or present.

> *Keep away from people who try to belittle your ambitions. Small people always do that, but the really great make you feel that you, too, can become great.*
> Mark Twain

Practice selective watching also—what we continually look at is vital. We need to be more selective about what we look at outside our lives. We should pick good role models to focus on, and spend time with them if they are accessible and if they'll let us. We should edit out of our TV watching anything that is too negative, realizing that it is food our brains will digest and give us back in negative attitudes or self-limiting beliefs.

> *Ask yourself,* What am I saying? What am I looking at and listening to? How does this affect the positive dream I want to build into reality?

Pay attention to what you mull over in your mind, turning it over and looking at it again and again. Memories or possibilities: take your pick. You choose what your own mind focuses on.

*People who say it cannot be done
should not interrupt those who are doing it.* (1)

Begin to talk like you're already living in your dream.

We have written down the declarations of our dream elements in Chapter 7, and our goals and action steps in Chapter 16. With these before us, we need to spend some time projecting ourselves into our future as if they were already accomplished, and we were already in the middle of that place, activity, relationship, position, and determine what we are feeling there. This requires three things: time, mental visualization and emotional involvement in what we see.

By now it's eminently obvious that none of the concepts of this book are complicated. The reason for going through these truths so meticulously is to lay out a step-by-step pathway *we can see ourselves walking*, while looking at the capabilities built into us that make it possible for us to walk them out. As we do these steps, information is being driven deeply into our very cells, into the subconscious strata of our minds where we are impacting our established belief systems and our heart's expectations.

We're not merely getting information that we may or may not already be familiar with, which is what most books provide. Nor are we advocating changing our outward behavior in certain ways and saying that's all it takes for success, which is another thing I have read in a number of "success books." If we concentrate on changing our core heart beliefs about ourselves, behavior changes are easier, and will become second-nature with time. The life changes we make can then be *permanent*. When the dysfunction of limiting beliefs is overridden by the truth about our amazing built-in capabilities and potentials, and we have the beginnings of an understanding of our purpose, we can begin to build that best life I keep talking about.

It is never too late to set new goals or dream new dreams. At 90, the architect Frank Lloyd Wright designed the Guggenheim Museum.

At seventy-eight years old, Benjamin Franklin invented bifocal spectacles. (2)

You are never too old to set another goal or to dream a new dream.
CS Lewis

When we begin dreaming new dreams, we will need to guard our fledgling new dreams carefully. Nourish and tend them. We all know better than to leave a baby alone unattended. Why would we leave unattended—or unfed—something so critical to our success in life and our ultimate happiness as our dreams?

We have two lifestyle choices

We said that our life is a structure, and as with all structures, it will have certain ways it will act, behave and work. There are two basic *structural patterns* people have: One is steadily advancing forward and the second is a one-step-forward-two-steps-back pattern. (3)

"Advancing is a life structure in which the success you have achieved becomes the platform for future success.
You can build momentum over time, and the sum total of your life experiences leads you forward."
Robert Fritz

Which pattern our life follows depends largely on our focus, and on who's in charge of the game plan. Think about it: if we look backward with regret, we are admitting we may have made a mistake, and may not have gotten it right the first time around. If we live in regret, we'll live in failure. All we will see is the unsatisfactory outcome of past situations, and that will be our focus, which will continue to pull past failures into our future. Don't let your past be in charge of your future. Backward is the wrong direction for your life focus.

Also don't focus on what is lacking, or what you *don't see* in your life. Self-pity will kill your dream. It is not a healthy place to live in. continuing self-pity is an indication that grieving has not been completed somewhere. Finish the grieving process, rename your life events with the good that came out of them and focus ahead on your dreams. Focus on what you want to see *added* to your life.

A wrong focus can lead to fear. And fear has the ability to paralyze us, and *hold* our focus on a bad expectation. Fear comes in all shapes and sizes, and a number of them are so common as to seem "socially acceptable." The extreme of panic is one end of a pendulum swing of fear, but the other end is worry, anxiety, apprehension, caution, a nagging "uncertainty" about the future, etc. The problem with fear in any of its sizes or shades is that ALL of them deplete our hope.

Go where you need to go to be who you're destined to be.

Maintaining a forward focus

If your pathway (i.e. your life) is confusing you, back off and get a fresh perspective. I found a photo of a sign on the internet, posted on a roadside, and it read "Absolutely nothing—next 22 miles." Don't you wish life provided signs like this? But real life doesn't encourage the use of autopilot.

Instead, like another sign I found, life is full of misdirection: "CAUTION This sign has SHARP EDGES Do not touch the edges of this sign." And then in *very* tiny print under that: "Also, the bridge is out ahead." We have to decide what's important. If the path we're following comes to a sudden end, we should go back to the last place we had multiple options and re-evaluate our possibilities. Look at the choices we made and the options we still have before us. Take the fresh-start courage that mercy gives and start in again. Go where you need to go to be who you're destined to be.

Practical aspects that build forward momentum

Do I wait for circumstances to overwhelm me? Or do I work actively and sow actions that will make me ready for the future, and will keep me from being overwhelmed? That's called proactivity. It could be the difference between sitting on your roof while the water level creeps higher and higher, waiting for rescue from floodwaters, or participating in preventative measures before the storms hit and the floods come. Be proactive.

Be flexible. Be alert in your "now" and be willing to adjust plans you've already made. Pay attention to what you are seeing, and if something isn't working, be willing to change it.

Pay attention to your decisions. There are no unimportant choices. All choices are crossroad moments, and there are some freeways we can't just get off easily when we finally realize we've made the wrong choice and we're in the wrong place, headed away from our best life and our dreams.

Pick your battles. Stop beating your head against brick walls. Only take on those things that have to do with moving your dream forward. Let the battles you are never going to walk away from whole go unfought (by you, anyway) for awhile. Come back to resolve those things later, when you are stronger from your fulfilled dreams.

Reposition yourself for success whenever you feel uncertain. Rehearse your dream out loud every day.

As you think about your dream it will grow in your mind. When it does, push what you see a little further and set some new SMART goals. As you grow, your goals should be changing. Put new action steps to them whenever you've accomplished the steps you had, or your goals have stretched bigger. Your action plan is flexible; it should also grow with you. Keep calmly analyzing and adjusting what you are doing with your dream in center focus. Make adjustments whenever you need to incorporate an increased understanding of your dream components.

> *Start by doing what's necessary, then do what's possible,*
> *and suddenly you are doing the impossible.*
>
> St. Francis of Assisi

Look at everything through the rose-colored glasses of your life purpose as you concentrate on building your dream. Look at things around you, in your life, and in your heart with this filter: Will this help me get to my best life (my dream) or not?

Do something every day towards your dream. Only you can determine if you're making satisfactory progress toward your dream. Always remember to break down your action steps until you have *do-able* steps that you know-to-your-bones there is no excuse not to start doing *today*. Put some pressure on yourself to DO what's in your action plan.

What to avoid

Avoid things and people that pull the wrong responses out of your memory. Ignore the attempts of people to criticize, belittle, or misunderstand your dream efforts. Limit who you hang around with—if they're dreamstealers, do they need to be in your life? The best revenge is to live a wildly successful and healthy life, and let the dreamstealers who hurt us suffer jealousy as they look at our happy, thriving lives.

Deal with the things *you have control over* that affect your hope: what you watch on TV, what you read, what you listen to on the radio. Ask yourself: What else do I have control over? What should I avoid?

Whenever you see what's bound to be a really bad time looming up on your horizon and looking unavoidable, this is the time to put your trust in God. When I teach The Permission to Dream Book, at this point I refer to a picture I saw of a big tanker heading into the storm that became Hurricane Katrina. Sometimes circumstances land on us with both feet, and we can't go around them. That's the time we should do as the Bible says: "Cast (throw) all your cares upon Him, for He cares for you." (4)

Commit all the things outside your control into God's care. He's even more invested in your success than you are.

☙❧ Chapter 18: Get the Help You Need

> *Just as your car runs more smoothly and requires less energy to go faster and farther when the wheels are in perfect alignment, you perform better when your thoughts, feelings, emotions, goals, and values are in balance.*
>
> Brian Tracy

A right focus helps us maintain balance. Our lives work best when our thoughts, feelings, emotions, goals and values are in balance.

A right focus is looking forward at our future life through the filter of our purpose. Live forward. It's the right direction in which to think and imagine, to aim, to dream. We are actually created for this lifestyle, and we function best in it. A forward focus is the realm of possibilities and increasing hope.

God himself only does forward. God is such a good planner, and so extremely intelligent, that he's already worked out the best way to get what he wants done before he makes a single move. It's like a well-planned-out assembly line, where every part is finessed for maximum effectiveness and efficiency before the ON button is pushed for the first time. He figures out every contingency of the moves other people can make, and how to keep his plan moving forward no matter what choices anyone else makes. You wouldn't want to play chess with God. He'd *always* win.

Build a "Dream Team"

We need each other, and no one is capable of fulfilling their dreams all by themselves. If you *can* do your dream all by yourself, you're doing yourself an injustice by dreaming too small. Dream a bigger dream. And then start looking for the people and resources that will enable you to fulfill it.

Interview everyone

Interview everyone you meet for potential candidates. Ask yourself:

What kind of people will I need to accomplish my dream?

Build your dream team around your strengths. What facets of your dream are you the strongest in doing? For example: If you are the one who sees things far off and inspires other people to go with you, are you also detail-oriented, and very organized? If accounting is not your strong suit, you're going to need to recruit an accountant. You may require legal advice in getting your dream established. You look for the skills you're "weak" in to be supplied from the people on your team.

When you have a beginning idea of the kind of people you need on your team, then ask yourself about everyone you meet, and everyone already in your life: Does this person believe in me, and will they help me make my dream happen?

Actively look for resources

Actively look for the resources that will contribute to your dream. Look at everything around you with a view to "will this help me or not?" But don't stress about not having what is needed. Keep your eyes on the dream statements you're declaring as though you're already living in them, and keep declaring them with strong positive feeling like you're already there and it's a done deal. You're building your confidence in your dream being accomplished with every visualization and declaration. Then watch for the resources to begin showing up in your life.

Make lists

Make lists as you discover things you will need and as you find them. Continually be thinking: how can I fit this into my dream? Is this necessary for my dream?

Evaluate everything

Evaluate everything in your life through the filter of your purpose. Analyze what you see in successful people. Watch for people who are doing similar things. Try to figure out what they are doing that works for them. And ask yourself if it's something you can start doing too. If it's too difficult right now, put it on your list as something to work toward.

Be sure God is part of your "dream team"

The strongest advocate for your success is God. He's the smartest and best success coach in existence. Make sure he's on your team.

None of us can dream a truly big dream *without* God's help. We all need the fresh starts of mercy. Some of us have sat and cried with the aching need for a fresh start. God is the source of fresh starts; He is the God of mercy. It's a part of who God is—He makes everything new. The beginning of the Bible describes how he made the new earth. At the end of the Bible, practically the last words of God are "I make everything new." The Bible says "if any man be in Christ, he is a new creature: old things are passed away; behold, all things are become new." (1) There is no deep, dark and mysterious meaning for "all things" here—it means *ALL things*, with no exceptions. What is worn and frayed in your life that needs some refreshing to make it like new again?

No one but God will ever know you so completely, and accept you so wholeheartedly. No one else can be with you every time you have a need. No one else can coach you so efficiently into your dream. You can ask his help freely. The super-intelligent mind that thought up 200 billion galaxies is more than sufficient to solve *any* issue that faces you.

If He can hold the whole world in His hands, don't you think He's strong enough to hold you? When your own heart fails you, it's more than nice to have someone BIG who believes in you. "My flesh and my heart fail all the time, but God is the strength of my heart and my portion forever." (2)

Pay attention

Pay careful attention to everything that is happening around you. Be continually asking yourself: How does this fit into my dream? You never know where or when a door of opportunity is going to open. They don't just announce themselves with a shout of "I'm here: your next golden opportunity!" Opportunities will often look like adverse circumstances when they first show up in our lives. Knowing this can take a lot of the fear out of our lives, and allow our life to be a positive adventure. If we have asked God for help with our dreams, we should know that he is completely good, and he will turn everything that happens to us around to our good. (3) So we can be optimistic and look forward to whatever comes. This kind of thinking actually helps us to see more of our dream as it's approaching. A positive mindset is a huge asset in itself.

Start-overs are okay. Quitting is not.

We see most clearly through our glasses of purpose when we are looking in the light of fresh mercy. Be excruciatingly honest with yourself.

When frustrations, doubts, fears begin to move you, or you lose temporary sight of your purpose, give yourself a mental push in the direction of another *fresh start*. Whenever you're out of the "mercy zone," get back in with all speed. For example, when you identify something you just said that resonates in your heart, and it wasn't pretty, ask God to help you change it. When you fall down and hurt yourself, you deal with it, washing it off and putting antiseptic and Band-Aids on it, right? Give your heart issues the same careful attention. It's what you are thinking in your heart that defines you, whether you're aware of what your heart is saying or not. (4)

When you blow it, don't beat yourself up about it. Remember God has an unlimited supply of mercy-fresh-starts for those who love him. Mercy provides the atmosphere of fresh starts. Mercy repositions us in good standing with God. Every time we get confused, off course, make a wrong step or whatever, we get our freshness and hope back by reconnecting to God. Make a fresh start. Freshness is a beautiful place of renewed hope and courage.

We should focus on keeping a right relationship with God, and continually be trying to see things more clearly through our purpose. The Bible says, "Commit everything you do to the Lord. Trust him and He will help you." (5) Put your dreams in God's hands.

Cultivate the mindset of hope—be like the farmer, who sows seeds *knowing* there will come a harvest in due time. Keep working the garden of your dream. Encourage yourself with the inevitability of success as you work the dream process. Our enthusiastic declarations are exactly like planting seeds, watering them in, and tilling the ground as they grow—there *will be* a resulting crop of new behavior, new life perspectives, and new successes.

Give your imagination freedom to fly forward into increasingly more possibilities, by refusing to look behind you or dwell on what you have already lived through. Talk your dream out loud every day to yourself, like you're already living in it. Say something to yourself about it first thing in the morning when you wake up, and again last thing at night before sleeping. Sow some visualizing time into your daily routine. Give yourself time to see your dream vividly, to the point where you can feel what it's like to be already there in it, living it. When you really get there, it should seem comfortably familiar.

Life with a dream becomes simpler: it's all forward movement toward our dream and everything that happens that seems adverse can be summarized as exercises to grow stronger. The mind is like your muscles—thought patterns grow stronger with repetition. Practice setting goals. Practice self-awareness; keep listening to what your heart is saying. Practice your new strategies for success. Build your support systems. Live proactively: keep building your dream.

Declaration #18: I can and do ask my God for help with my dreams
Declaration #19: I will use as many fresh starts as I need.

ೞೞ Chapter 19: My Absolute Rights

The biggest adventure you can take is to live the life of your dreams.
Oprah Winfrey

Woven throughout Permission to Dream are a series of absolute truths. These are rock-solid truth concerning abilities we each own unconditionally. No one can limit our use of these abilities unless we allow it. They are completely true for us, and they will work 100% for each of us.

As with everything else, these capabilities we completely own come in seed form, and we have to practice them to allow them to grow in our lives. Undoubtedly I own a number of things in my attic but if I don't pull them down and incorporate them into my life, what use are they?

The first truth is the absolute right to hope. We've seen how hope is affected by the disappointments of life, and we've looked at the process of building hope stronger again. No one can keep us from hoping. People try, but hope is intensely personal, and it begins with an act of will—"I will put my hope in…" If in our putting, we put our hope in God, all of our hoping works better. He's a world-class catalyst for positivity.

Declare: It is my absolute right to have forward-focusing, positive, strong and vibrant hope.

It is also my absolute right to imagine. No one can stop us from exercising our imagination; that is, unless we allow it. When we begin to imagine, our first forays into the world of possibilities may seem pretty lame and small. But don't let that stop you. Keep pushing imagination until the new realms of possibilities we are imagining blow our minds. Live in possibilities; it's incredibly conducive to increasing hope, and it gives us more potential choices for our future.

Declare: It is my absolute right to use my unlimited imagination to think "new" instead of "familiar," and imagine possibilities.

169

Hoping and imagining new possibilities will make exercising our third absolute right easier—it is our right to choose for ourselves. If we are in a position where there are restraints we don't like, we can choose to imagine and dream a better place for ourselves, to enable us to survive the restricted place. If there are no outward pressures restraining us, and we can exercise our right to choose freely, then we can join choice to imagination and begin to dream that best life I keep talking about.

Declare: It is my absolute right to choose, and by my own choice to build new, good things in my life.

It is an absolute right also for us to dive into our imaginations with both feet, and not just picture, but see and feel what it would be like to live in that place. We can try our imagined places on for size, before we throw ourselves into the process of going there. If we do this well, when we get to our dream life, it will have the benefit of already being familiar. The fear of the unknown will have been removed.

Declare: It is my absolute right to visualize what I imagine, in vivid detail.

By doing these things, we are being efficient with our own time and resources. We can do the trial and error process mentally rather than putting our efforts and resources into exploring our possibilities in linear time. We can mentally experience what it feels like to live in the dream we're imagining for ourselves without the tiniest bit of circumstance changing. This makes dreaming *completely workable* right now, from wherever we are.

Declare: It is my absolute right to feel what it's like to be already living my vividly imagined dream, before anything visibly changes.

Our first dreams may not be very big. One young lady I taught said "I just want to get my driver's license," when I asked for a statement of what her best life looked like. She has graduated the Union Gospel Mission program since that day. Today that lady is in college and doing very well. She's working toward a degree that will enable her to counsel women recovering from addiction, and her dreams are so much bigger than merely getting a driver's license. It is our absolute right to continually dream bigger and bigger. There are no limits on how big we may dream.

Declare: It is my absolute right to dream HUGE dreams, even beyond anything that's ever been imagined before. There are no impossible dreams.

It is also our absolute right to connect with God in this process. No one can stop us from reaching out to God, and asking for his help in accomplishing our dreams. He actually loves dreamers, and the Bible says "Nothing is too hard for God." (1) You may find when God gets involved in your dream, it gets even bigger.

Declare: It is my absolute right to ask my God to help me accomplish my dreams. Nothing is too hard for my God.

And lastly, once we've connected with God, we have access to as many fresh starts as it takes. We've seen that fresh starts are part of receiving God's mercy, and that he has an inexhaustible supply of mercy for us. There's no cut-off point. Every time in the process of walking out our dreams when we get tired or discouraged, reach for that fresh-start-feeling. It's invigorating.

Declare: It is my absolute right to as many fresh starts as I need. God's mercy is new every morning.

Because these truths are *absolute*, they hold completely true for everyone. These absolute truths together make a solid platform on which to stand and reach forward for our best life. This platform may be the key that makes it possible to get there. And the best part is that these truths are part of the way human beings are made—all human beings. You have these rights, the same as I do. No one is excluded; they work for everyone. If we use these rights freely, they put an "I CAN" in us, an inner confidence that when opportunity arrives to step into my dream, *I can do it*. Powerful!

ೞೞ Chapter 20: Don't stop until I get there

> *There are no impossible dreams.*
>
> Glenna Salsbury

The last declaration in <u>The Permission to Dream Book</u> is:
I WILL keep moving forward until I get my dreams.

The purpose of this book has been to build a strong platform of renewed hope and confidence under our dreams, so we can move into our future with a good expectation, and the ground will no longer be able to drop out suddenly from under our feet.

We said it before: it's a lifestyle choice. We can either spend our whole lives moving from one crisis to another, or we can choose to deliberately build our dreams and live proactively.

We don't all start life on an even plain. Few of us are born with silver spoons in our mouth. The life journeys may have been rocky and difficult that brought us to this present moment, but this is a day and a place of fresh starts. It is never too late to start building or rebuilding our dreams, and focusing forward into possibilities. If we have lost our dreams somewhere along the way, reclaim them, and calmly begin rebuilding.

The only person who can keep you from fulfilling your dreams is YOU. Imagine possibilities. Make new choices. Speak them out loud with strong feeling every day. Build your confidence. These are the building blocks of new dreams, a tried-and-true formula for success. Work it. Live your dream!

Let's review the process of dreaming one last time. Think of these dream components as a formula that has been well-proven; it works, giving consistent positive results.

Hope gives us the "I CAN" for our dreams. Hope is what we live for. Hope is what we expect to satisfy us. Hope is what we believe is possible for us. This is because the ultimate and unlimited source of hope is God, to whom all things are possible. "Now the God of hope fill you with all joy and peace in believing, that you may abound in hope, through the power of the Holy Spirit." (1)

Imagination gives us the WHAT, the unlimited possibilities for our dreams. Imagination is our unlimited absolute right and ability to think creatively.

> *I am enough of an artist to draw freely upon my imagination.*
> *Imagination is more important than knowledge.*
> *Knowledge is limited. Imagination encircles the world.*
> Albert Einstein

This is the voice of one of the world's greatest scientists. If you can't believe God's word on it yet, believe science. The creative capacity in us is unlimited. The only limitations that can stop us are our own deep-set beliefs.

Our imagination works in two directions—backwards into memory and forward into creative possibilities. I can't stress enough how important this is—FOCUS FORWARD. What you focus on is what you expect, and what you expect is ultimately what you get. Focus on your future dreams.

> *If you can imagine it you can create it.*
> *If you can dream it, you can become it.*
> William Arthur Ward

Choice is our absolute right to choose for ourselves. Choice gives us ownership of our imagined possibilities, and turns a choice into my door of opportunity. We make our own opportunities by our choices. Self-awareness enables us to make choices without circumstances or feelings getting in the way of our judgment. Use self-awareness to stand apart from the pain and get some fresh perspective, so we are able to make new choices that will allow the dream process to work freely in our lives.

Speaking our visualized dream out loud repeatedly with strong feeling calls it to us, builds our confidence in what we are saying, and strengthens us to step into it when the opportunity presents itself. You can anticipate what you will feel when you succeed...use *that feeling* before you get there when you're rehearsing your dream declarations. Our dream declarations may start out as pure imagination, but with repetition, they will become compellingly strong.

Absolute rights

Your absolute rights are yours as a human being. No one can take these away from you, no matter what circumstances may occur. You cannot lose them, but you can refuse to use them. You can *give* your rights to someone else, but why would you want to?

Use your absolute rights to keep your strong confidence in your dreams everywhere you go.

Example: The need to regroup and put the solid foundation of confidence back under your feet can happen anywhere, at any time. Start from the beginning and rebuild it with the absolute truths that you stand on. "I'm still breathing, so I have hope. My hope is growing. I have an unlimited ability to imagine. I am imagining possibilities.

"I have the absolute right to choose, and I choose to dream. I have the absolute right to see myself living in my dreams and feel what it's like before I get there. I can and do ask for and receive God's help. I have as many fresh starts as I need. Okay, I'm good to go now."

Some last thoughts I want to emphasize

Don't ever look at circumstances and obstacles the same way again. We all have obstacles to our dreams and our purpose. Our choice is either to focus on the obstacles or to look beyond them to whatever part of our purpose we can see. And continue making declarations with strong feeling—the obstacles will start to disappear, and soon our view of our purpose will be what commands our attention again.

Get comfortable with who you are. Do the online personality tests. The Bible says: "He that is getting wisdom loves his own soul." (2) We don't love what we're not intimately acquainted with.

> *What you think of me is none of my business.*
> *What is most important is what I think of myself.*
>
> Robert Kiyosaki

Always look at life through your new "reality glasses." Keep your eyes fixed on your purpose. You'll find it forms the core of your dreams. Use the corrected prescription of your life purpose to give you a clear vision for your future.

When you're wearing the glasses of your purpose, it works two ways—you see clearly, and people see your purpose on you too. And when you look at yourself through your purpose, you see yourself differently. Don't sell yourself short. If you are human, there is capacity for greatness in you.

As for finding lost dreams:

Your heart answers to you. The Bible tells us "As in water face answers to face, so the heart of man to man." (3) Search your heart for parts of lost dreams and ask God's help in recovering your forgotten dreams. Deal with anything and everything your heart shows you that might reach out and attach itself to your dream, i.e. limitations, self-doubt, fear, etc.

Deal with everything that could come out of your past and overwhelm you as you are pursuing your dream. Rename your signpost moments and put them to rest. When you remember a childhood dream, examine it for the seeds of life-long dreams. Then pick up where the childhood dream left off and begin building on the life-long dream that still resonates in you.

Dealing with the pain.

Don't choose to continue in your grief any longer than necessary to heal from it. Finish the grieving process. Remember that forgiving is necessary to release YOU from the ball and chain of that past trauma and its emotional load.

Forgive for your own sake. Keep moving forward in the grieving process at your own speed. You will get to the end of grief if you don't stop, and you will continue your deep healing along the way.

Don't let fear stop you from moving forward into your dreams. Do what you need to do. Do it afraid, but do it. That's real courage.

Actually, I don't think lack of courage is the problem for many of us. I think the problem was not knowing what our options were, and also believing the limitations and false labels put on us. We are here, so we're survivors. That shows a strength of will that will stand us in good stead if we re-direct it forward now to building our dreams.

Only she who attempts the absurd can achieve the impossible.
Robin Morgan

The saying accredited to St. Francis of Assisi holds true for both men and for women—we start doing the necessary things, then move into the "harder" improbable things, and without realizing it at some point we'll step into doing what we used to think was impossible. Put aside pride and go for it. Who cares if it didn't work in the past? We have better tools for this next run at it.

The things you want are always possible;
It is just that the way to get them is not always apparent.
Les Brown

Don't try to walk your road alone. Ask for the help you need, from the people in your life and from your God. Ask God to show you the fastest way to your dreams. The Bible says "If any of you lacks wisdom, let him ask God, who gives generously to all without reproach, and it will be given him." (4)

God only does straight forward. However, to our eyes, the straight path he sets us often looks like the convoluted twists of switchback curves. Trust him anyway. He's committed to us. "He that spared not his own Son, but delivered him up for us all, how shall he not with him also freely give us all things?" (5) Trust God to show you the fastest way. Isn't the fastest way the straightest when it comes right down to it?

> *Go confidently in the way of your dreams.*
> *Live the life you've imagined.*
>
> Henry David Thoreau

In closing, when you see someone at the top of a mountain, know and understand that they didn't just fall there. Determine to yourself to keep moving forward and upward one step at a time, and don't stop until you reach the fulfillment of your dreams and the top of your own mountain.

Take this last encouragement from me—You have all the resources you need to explore the unlimited possibilities before you. It's the absolute truth: You can do it.

Footnotes

Chapter 1

1—p. 16 Collins English Dictionary – complete & Unabridged 10th Edition 2009, William Collins sons & Co. Ltd. 1979, n1986 Harper Collins Publishers 1998, 2000, 2003, 2005, 2006, 2007, 2009
http://dictionary.reference.com/browse/sabotage?r=75&src=ref&ch=dic

2—p. 17 I used concepts if not actual words from some or all of the following websites on self-sabotage:
    a—**http://soulhiker.com/2011/07/self-sabotage-the-subconscious-mindovercoming-self-sabotaging-behavior/**
    b—**http://www.psychologytoday.com/basics/self-sabotage**
    c—**http://www.psychologytoday.com/blog/evolution-the-self/201101/the-programming-self-sabotage-pt-3-the-logical-illogic-the-psycho-log**
    d—**http://aschwartz.hubpages.com/hub/What-Is-Self-Sabotage**
    e—**http://stress.about.com/od/selfknowledgeselftests/a/self_sabotage.htm**
    f—**http://www.terrilevine.com/articles/sabotaging-behaviors.htm**

3—p. 17 Excerpt from a 2006 National Geographic online article on the brain.

4—p. 18 image from
http://www.exchange3d.com/images/uploads/aff2794/human%20body.jpg

5—p. 18 The Heart's Code: Tapping the Wisdom and Power of Our Heart Energy by Paul Pearsall, Ph.D. Broadway Books, New York 1998, p. 69

6—p. 19 Everything You Need to Know to Feel Go(o)d by Candace B. Pert, Ph.D. with Nancy Marriott, Hay House, Inc., 2006, p.46-47

7—p. 19 The Brain That Changes Itself: Stories of Personal Triumph from the Frontiers of Brain Science by Norman Doidge M.D., Penguin Group Inc., NY, 2007

8—p. 19 **http://science.nationalgeographic.com/science/health-and-human-body/human-body/mind-brain/#page=1** "Beyond the Brain" Written by James Shreeve, republished from the pages of *National Geographic* magazine

9—p. 19 Molecules of Emotion: The Science Behind Mind-Body Medicine by Candace B. Pert, PH.D., Scribner, 1997, p.185

10—p. 20 <u>Molecules of Emotion: The Science Behind Mind-Body Medicine</u> by Candace B. Pert, PH.D., Scribner, 1997, p.187-188

11—p. 21 **http://www.mindpoweruntold.com/2010/03/how-our-mind-works-conscious-and.html**

12—p. 23 <u>Blink: The Power of Thinking Without Thinking</u> by Malcolm Gladwell, Little, Brown and Company, 2005, p. 11

13—p. 23 The 1986 movie: <u>Short Circuit</u>, year, directed by John Badham, Number 5 voice by Tim Blaney.

14—p. 23 <u>The Biology of Belief</u> by Bruce H. Lipton, Ph. D., Hay House, Inc., 2005, p. 136

15—p. 23 Excerpt from National Geographic's website: **http://kids.nationalgeographic.com/kids/stories/spacescience/brain/**

16—p. 23 <u>Blink: The Power of Thinking Without Thinking</u> by Malcolm Gladwell, Little, Brown and Company, 2005, p. 11

17—p. 24 **http://en.wikipedia.org/wiki/Unconscious_mind**

18—p. 24 **http://en.wikipedia.org/wiki/Unconscious_mind**

19—p. 24 <u>The 4:8 Principle: The Secret to a Joy-Filled Life</u> by Tommy Newberry, Tyndale House Publishers, Inc., 2007, p. 135

20—p. 26 <u>The Heart's Code: Tapping the Wisdom and Power of Our Heart Energy</u> by Paul Pearsall, Ph.D. Broadway Books, New York 1998, p. 4-5

21—p. 26 Excerpt from **http://www.channel14.com/health/microsites/W/who_gets_the_heart/**

22—p. 26 <u>The Heart's Code: Tapping the Wisdom and Power of Our Heart Energy</u> by Paul Pearsall, Ph.D. Broadway Books, New York 1998, p. 5

23—p. 27 <u>The Heart's Code: Tapping the Wisdom and Power of Our Heart Energy</u> by Paul Pearsall, Ph.D. Broadway Books, New York 1998, p.12 In the book's footnote on this quote, the author says: The field of energy cardiology was named and developed by Gary E. Schwartz, Ph.D., and Linda G. Russek, Ph.D. They first proposed their theories about an interdisciplinary approach to study how the concept of energy and information conveyed within that energy applies to the cardiovascular systems in "Energy Cardiology: A Dynamic Systems Approach for Integrating Conventional and Alternative Medicine," *Advances* Vol. 12 (1996): pp. 4-24.

24—p. 31 Collins English Dictionary – complete & Unabridged 10th Edition 2009, William Collins sons & Co. Ltd. 1979, n1986 Harper Collins Publishers 1998, 2000, 2003, 2005, 2006, 2007, 2009
http://dictionary.reference.com/browse/hope?s=t

25—p. 32 The Bible, Ecclesiastes 9:4 NLT

26—p. 32 The Bible, Romans 4:18

Chapter 2

1—p. 34 The Bible, Genesis 8.22

2—p. 34 The Bible, 1 Corinthians 9:10 NET

3—p. 35 image from **http://php.beenegarter.com/signup/ BG%20Portal%20Info/Images/Sprout.jpg**

4—p. 37 The Bible, Jeremiah 29:11

5—p. 37 The Bible, Matthew 6:21

6—p. 38 **http://thechampionsheart.com/getting-out-of-your-head-and-into-your-heart-3-keys**
By Mitchell Dahood, M.A., founder of The Champions Heart

7—p. 39 Excerpt from: **http://www.boardofwisdom.com/default.asp? start=51&topic=1005&listname=sports**

8—p. 39 The Bible, Psalms 43:5

Chapter 3

1—p. 41 "The Believing Child" (1970), a short story by Zenna Henderson in <u>Holding Wonder</u>, Avon Books, 1972. ISBN: 0-380-01250-0

2—p. 42 Collins English Dictionary – complete & Unabridged 10th Edition 2009, William Collins sons & Co. Ltd. 1979, n1986 Harper Collins Publishers 1998, 2000, 2003, 2005, 2006, 2007, 2009
http://dictionary.reference.com/browse/reproductive+imagination

3—p. 42 Collins English Dictionary – complete & Unabridged 10th Edition 2009, William Collins sons & Co. Ltd. 1979, n1986 Harper Collins Publishers 1998, 2000, 2003, 2005, 2006, 2007, 2009
http://dictionary.reference.com/browse/creative+imagination

4—p. 44 **http://www.bri.ucla.edu/bri_who/Directors_Message.asp**, from the Director's Message, by Chris Evans, Director of the Brain Research Institute UCLA

5—p. 45 Collins English Dictionary – complete & Unabridged 10th Edition 2009, William Collins sons & Co. Ltd. 1979, n1986 Harper Collins Publishers 1998, 2000, 2003, 2005, 2006, 2007, 2009
http://dictionary.reference.com/browse/impossible?s=t

6—p. 46 **http://inventors.about.com/library/inventors/bledison.htm**

7—p. 47 **http://listverse.com/2008/04/05/10-great-inventions-that-should-be-invented/**

8—p. 49-51 **http://www.bibleprobe.com/tess.htm**

Chapter 4

1—p. 53 The Mind & The Brain: Neuroplasticity and the Power of Mental Force by Jeffrey M. Schwartz, M.D., and Sharon Begley, Harper Collins Publishers, 2003, pp. 362-363

2—p. 54 Chicken Soup for the Soul by Jack Canfield and Mark Victor Hansen, pp. 191-195

Chapter 5

1—p. 56 The 7 Habits of Highly Effective People by Stephen R Covey, Free Press, A Division of Simon & Schuster, Inc. NY, 1989, p. 72

2—p. 57 The 7 Habits of Highly Effective People by Stephen R Covey, Free Press, A Division of Simon & Schuster, Inc. NY, 1989.

3—p. 57 Excerpt from National Geographic online article on the brain.

4—p. 58 The Bible, Proverbs 14:30 NKJV

5—pp. 60-61 The 7 Habits of Highly Effective: People: Powerful Lessons in Personal Change by Stephen R Covey, Free Press, A Division of Simon & Schuster, Inc. NY, 1989, p. 69-70

6—p. 63 The 7 Habits of Highly Effective: People: Powerful Lessons in Personal Change by Stephen R Covey, Free Press, A Division of Simon & Schuster, Inc. NY, 1989, p 70

7—p. 64 Molecules of Emotion by Candace B. Pert, Ph.D., Scribner, 1997 p. 141

8—p. 65 Man's Search for Meaning by Viktor E. Frankl, Beacon Press, 1959, p. 86

Chapter 7

1—p. 69 The Bible, Proverbs 18:21

2—p. 70 Everything You Need to Know to Feel Go(o)d by Candace B. Pert, Ph.D. with Nancy Marriott, Hay House, Inc., 2006, p. 111

3—p. 71 The Bible, Matthew 12:24

4—p. 71 The Bible, Proverbs 4:23

5—p. 73, 76 Chicken Soup for the Soul: Living Your Dreams by Jack Canfield and Mark Victor Hansen, Health Communications, Inc., August 12, 2003, p. 30-32

6—p. 73 The 4:8 Principle: The Secret to a Joy-Filled Life by Tommy Newberry, Tyndale House Publishers, Inc., 2007, p. 135

7—p. 74 The Bible, Proverbs 18:21

8—p. 74 The Brain That Changes Itself: Stories of Personal Triumph from the Frontiers of Brain Science by Norman Doidge M.D., Penguin Group Inc., NY, 2007, pp. 200, 203-204

9—p. 74 <u>The Brain That Changes Itself: Stories of Personal Triumph from the Frontiers of Brain Science</u> by Norman Doidge M.D., Penguin Group Inc., NY, 2007, p. 204

Chapter 8

1—p. 82 The Bible, Joel 2:25 KJV

2—p. 85 Gabriella-Paige
www.boardofwisdom.com/default.asp?topic... Gabriella-Paige+

Chapter 9

1—p. 90 Collins English Dictionary – complete & Unabridged 10th Edition 2009, William Collins sons & Co. Ltd. 1979, n1986 Harper Collins Publishers 1998, 2000, 2003, 2005, 2006, 2007, 2009
http://dictionary.reference.com/browse/truth?s=t

2—p. 91 <u>Creating</u> and <u>Your Life as Art</u> by Robert Fritz
http://www.robertfritz.com/index.php?content=principles

3— p. 92 <u>The 4:8 Principle: The Secret to a Joy-Filled Life</u> by Tommy Newberry, Tyndale House Publishers, Inc., 2007, p. 135

4—p. 93 <u>Creating</u> and <u>Your Life as Art</u> by Robert Fritz
http://www.robertfritz.com/index.php?content=principles

Chapter 10

1—p. 95 Job 14:7-9 KJV

2—p. 96 The Bible, Proverbs 14:10 NKJV

3—p. 99 <u>7 Stages of Grief</u> by Jennie Wright, RN
http://www.recover-from-grief.com/7-stages-of-grief.html

4—p 100 The Bible, Psalms 30:5

5—p. 102 The Bible, Matthew 6:14-15

Chapter 11

1—p. 105 William James, US Pragmatist philosopher and psychologist (1842-1910) **http://www.quotationspage.com/quote/39749.html**

2—p. 106 Collins English Dictionary – complete & Unabridged 10th Edition 2009, William Collins sons & Co. Ltd. 1979, n1986 Harper Collins Publishers 1998, 2000, 2003, 2005, 2006, 2007, 2009 **http://dictionary.reference.com/browse/personality?s=t**

3—p. 111 The Bible, Proverbs 4:23

4—p. 113 The Bible, 2 Corinthians 5:17

Chapter 12

1—p. 115 The Bible, Colossians 1:16

2—p. 115 The Bible, Psalms 139:14

3—p. 115 The Bible, Ephesians 1:4

4—p. 119 The Bible, Proverbs 16:4

5-6—p. 119 The Bible, Romans 9:20-21 KJV

7—p. 120 The Bible, Revelations 4:11

8—p. 120 The Bible, Psalms 139:14

9—p. 122 The Bible, Isaiah 40:26

10—p. 123 The Bible, 1 Corinthians 6:20 KJV

11—p. 123-124 The Bible, Psalm 139:1-18, 23-24 NLT

12—p. 124 Everything You Need to Know to Feel Go(o)d by Candace B. Pert, Ph.D., Hay House, Inc., 2006, p. 13

Chapter 13

1—p. 128 The Bible, Jeremiah 29:11 ESV

2—p. 128 The Bible, Romans 8:28 NLT

3—p. 128 The Bible, Psalm 23:6

4—p. 128 Think and Grow Rich by Napoleon Hill, p.

5—p. 131 Everything You Need to Know to Feel Go(o)d by Candace B. Pert, Ph.D., Hay House, Inc., 2006, p. 48

Chapter 14

1—p. 136 The Bible, Phil 3:13-16 CJB

2—p. 138 Attributed to William Arthur Ward

3—p. 138 The Bible, Mark 9:23

4—p. 139 Unknown

Chapter 15

1—p. 147 The Bible, Psalm 43:5

2-3—p. 148 The Bible, Romans 10:17

4—p. 148 The Bible, Romans 15:13

Chapter 16

1—p. 151 Doran, G. T. (1981). There's a S.M.A.R.T. way to write management's goals and objectives. Management Review, Volume 70, Issue 11(AMA FORUM), pp. 35-36.

2—p. 152 Meyer, Paul J (2003). **"What would you do if you knew you couldn't fail? Creating S.M.A.R.T. Goals"**. *Attitude Is Everything: If You Want to Succeed Above and Beyond*. Meyer Resource Group, Incorporated, The. **ISBN 978-0-89811-304-4**.

3—p. 154 A message as published in the Wall Street Journal by United Technologies Corp.

Chapter 17

1—p. 159 Unknown

2—p. 160 The Brain That Changes Itself: Stories of personal Triumph from the Frontiers of Brain Science by Norman Doidge, M.D., Penguin Books, 2007, p. 257

3—p. 160 Creating and Your Life as Art by Robert Fritz
http://www.robertfritz.com/index.php?content=principles

4—p. 163 The Bible, 1 Peter 5:7

Chapter 18

1—p. 166 The Bible, 2 Corinthians 5:17

2—p. 166 The Bible, Psalms 73:26

3—p. 167 The Bible, Romans 8:28

4—p. 167 The Bible, Proverbs 23:7 KJV

5— p. 168 The Bible, Psalms 37:5 NLT

Chapter 19

1—p. 171 The Bible, Jeremiah 32:17

Chapter 20

1—p. 173 The Bible, Romans 15:13

2—p. 175 The Bible, Proverbs 19:8

3—p. 175 The Bible, Proverbs 27:19

4—p. 176 The Bible, James 1:5 ESV

5—p. 177 The Bible, Romans 8:32

Recommended Reading List

Listed alphabetically by title

Blink: The Power of Thinking Without Thinking by Malcolm Gladwell, Little, Brown and Company, NY, 2005

Chicken Soup for the Soul by Jack Canfield and Mark Victor Hansen, Health Communications, Inc., FL, 1993

Chicken Soup for the Soul: Living Your Dreams by Jack Canfield and Mark Victor Hansen, Health Communications, Inc., August 12, 2003

Everything You Need to Know to Feel Go(o)d by Candace B. Pert, Ph.D., Hay House, Inc., NY, 2006

Healing and the Mind by Bill Moyers, Doubleday, a division of Bantam Doubleday Dell Publishing Group, Inc. NY, 1993

Healing Words: The Power of Prayer and the Practice of Medicine by Larry Dossey, M.D., HarperSanFrancisco, a division of HarperCollins Publishers, NY, 1993

Inside the Brain: Revolutionary Discoveries of How the Mind Works by Ronald Kotulak, Andrews McMeel Publishing, MI, 1996

Man's Search for Meaning by Viktor E. Frankl, Pocket Books, a division of Simon & Schuster, Inc., NY, 1959

Mindsight: The New Science of Personal Transformation by Daniel J. Siegel, M.D, Bantam Books, NY, 2010

Molecules of Emotion: The Science Behind Mind-Body Medicine by Candace B. Pert, Ph.D., Scribner, NY, 1997

Of Two Minds: The Revolutionary Science of Dual-brain Psychology by Fredric Schiffer, M.D.,
The Free Press, NY, 1998

Pocket Guide to Interpersonal Neurobiology: An Integrative Handbook of the Mind by Daniel J. Siegel, W.W. Norton & Company, Inc., NY, 2012

Sight and sensibility: the ecopsychology of perception by Laura Sewall, Ph.D., Jeremy P. Tarcher/Putnam, a member of Penguin Putnam, NY, 1999

The 4:8 Principle: The Secret to a Joy-filled Life by Tommy Newberry, Tyndale House Publishers, Inc., IL, 2007

The 7 Habits of Highly Effective People by Stephen R Covey, Free Press, A Division of Simon & Schuster, Inc. NY, 1989

The Biology of Belief: Unleashing the Power of Consciousness, Matter & Miracles by Bruce H. Lipton, Ph.D., Hay House, Inc., NY, 2005

The Heart's Code: Tapping the Wisdom and Power of Our Heart Energy: The New Findings About Cellular Memories and Their Role in the Mind/Body/Spirit Connection by Paul Pearsall, Ph.D., Broadway Books, NY 1998

The Mind & The Brain: Neuroplasticity and the Power of Mental Force by Jeffrey M Schwartz, M.D., and Sharon Begley, HarperCollins Publishers, NY, 2003

The Mindful Brain: Reflection and Attunement in the Cultivation of Well-being by Daniel J. Siegel, W.W. Norton & Company, NY, 2007

The Owner's Manual for The Brain: Everyday Applications from Mind-Brain Research by Pierce J. Howard, Ph.D., Bard Press, TX, 2006

Think & Grow Rich by Napoleon Hill, Ballantine Books, NY, 1983

Timeless Healing: The Power and Biology of Belief by Herbert Benson, M.D., Fireside, NY, 1997